L. DAVID MARQUET

Turn the
Ship Around!

A TRUE STORY OF
TURNING FOLLOWERS INTO LEADERS

BUSINESS

PENGUIN BUSINESS

UK | USA | Canada | Ireland | Australia
India | New Zealand | South Africa

Penguin Business is part of the Penguin Random House group of companies
whose addresses can be found at global.penguinrandomhouse.com.

Originally published in the United States of America by Greenleaf Book Group Press
Published in the United States of America by Portfolio/Penguin, a member of
Penguin Group (USA) Inc. 2015
Published in Great Britain by Portfolio Penguin 2015
Published in Penguin Business 2019

017

Printed and bound in Great Britain by Clays Ltd, Elcograf S.p.A.

A CIP catalogue record for this book is available from the British Library

ISBN: 978-0-241-25094-5

www.greenpenguin.co.uk

MIX
Paper from
responsible sources
FSC® C018179

Penguin Random House is committed to a
sustainable future for our business, our readers
and our planet. This book is made from Forest
Stewardship Council® certified paper.

Turn the Ship Around!

'I don't know of a finer model of this kind of empowering leadership than Captain Marquet. And in the pages that follow you will find a model for your pathway'
Stephen R. Covey, author of *The 7 Habits of Highly Effective People*

'To say I'm a fan of David Marquet would be an understatement. I'm a fully fledged groupie. He is the kind of leader who comes around only once a generation. He is the kind of leader who doesn't just know how to lead, he knows how to build leaders. His ideas and lessons are invaluable to anyone who wants to build an organization that will outlive them'
Simon Sinek, optimist and author of *Start with Why*

'How do we release the intellect and initiative of each member of the organization toward a common purpose? Here's the answer: with fascinating storytelling and a deep understanding of what motivates and inspires. David Marquet provides leaders in the military, business and education a powerful vehicle that will delight, provoke and encourage them to act'
Michael P. Peters, president, St John's College, Santa Fe

'I owe a lot to Captain David Marquet, not only for turning the *Santa Fe* around during some REALLY bad times, but I learned many lessons on leadership from him that have been invaluable in my post-Navy life. I preach the three legs (control, competence, clarity) of Leader-Leader every day to empower my people and move the decisions to where the information lives. I used these principles to turn around the GE Dallas generator repair department that was in crisis when I arrived in 2010 and is now the best generator repair department in the GE network. Now I am tasked with turning around the Dallas steam turbine repair department'
Adam McAnally, steam turbine cell leader, GE Dallas Service Center, and former crew member, USS *Santa Fe*

'This terrific read actually provides new and valuable insights into how to lead. And nothing important gets done without leadership. Captain Marquet takes you through his life of learning how to lead and presents you with a winning formula: Not leader-follower, but leader-leader. It's about leading by getting others to take responsibility – and like it. It works for business, politics, and life'

'It's *The Hunt for Red October* meets Harvard Business School. *Turn the Ship Around!* is the consummate book on leadership for the Information Age – where unleashing knowledge-workers' intellectual capital is pivotal in optimizing organizational performance, from maximizing market share and minimizing customer churn to improving margins. Captain Marquet's thesis is a complete paradigm shift in leadership philosophy. This new approach to leadership is applicable in all industries and across all corporate functions. If you're an organizational behaviour or leadership expert or enthusiast, this book can have a substantial impact on you and your organization's ability to meet its goals'

'David Marquet's message in *Turn the Ship Around!* inspires the empowerment of engaged people and leadership at all levels. He encourages leaders to release energy, intellect and passion in everyone around them. *Turn the Ship Around!* challenges the paradigm of the hierarchical organization by revealing the process to tear down pyramids, create a flat organization and develop leaders, not followers'

'This is the story of Captain David Marquet's unprecedented experiment in the most rigid of environments – on the *Santa Fe*, a US Navy nuclear-powered submarine. He had the courage to operate counterculture, re-engineering the very definition of leadership accepted by the US Navy for as long as it has existed. He took huge risks to do this. The outcome was revolutionary – within a few short months, the crew of the *Santa Fe* went from worst to first. In today's information age, human capital is our most precious resource. It is the twenty-first-century weapon of choice. Captain David Marquet's experiment in leadership has far greater application to the entire business world. This is thought leadership'
Charlie Kim, founder and CEO, Next Jump, Inc.

'Leaders and managers face an increasingly complex world where precise execution, teamwork and enabling of talent are competitive advantages. David Marquet provides a blueprint, along with real-life examples and implementation mechanisms. Anyone who is charged with leading and making a difference needs to read this'
John Cooper, president and CEO, Invesco Distributors

'David Marquet's book discusses the "successful motivation" that provided his people with the energy to overcome difficult obstacles. The values that he imbued in his folks provided a burst of energy that positively energized them by satisfying their needs for achievement – providing appropriate recognition, providing a sense of belonging, developing self-esteem, permitting a feeling of control and permitting an ability to live up to appropriate standards. This type of leadership energizes the workforce and allows senior management to paint the future and light a path that takes the entire team to it. This is a must-read for all who desire good moral influence on the workforce!'
Vice Admiral Al Konetzni (USN, ret.), former Pacific Fleet submarine commander

'The legacy of a commanding officer, or the leader of any organization, is how well the organization performs after he/she departs and the subsequent motivation, success and institutional contribution of those next-generation leaders who are trained and developed. Read *Turn the Ship Around!* and you will learn how to build enduring high performers who can't wait to get to work'

Admiral Thomas B. Fargo (USN, ret.), former commander, US Pacific Command, and chairman, Huntington Ingalls Industries

'Captain Marquet's compelling leadership journey inspires each of us to imagine a world where every human being is intellectually engaged and fully committed to solving our toughest challenges. If it can be done on a nuclear submarine, it can be done everywhere. *Turn the Ship Around!* delivers a brilliant message'

Liz Wiseman, author of *Multipliers: How the Best Leaders Make Everyone Smarter*

'What I learned from and with David Marquet is that developing a bottom-up, Leader-Leader culture produces highly empowered people and highly effective teams. It worked on a nuclear submarine and it worked in the mountains of Afghanistan. That said, cultivating a Leader-Leader culture is much easier said than done because you must overturn almost everything people grow up thinking and learning about leadership'

Captain (Sel) Dave Adams, USN, former Weapons Officer, USS *Santa Fe*, Khost Province PRT commander and commanding officer, USS *Santa Fe*

'David Marquet was handpicked to turn around a struggling submarine crew. With leadership and character he not only turned a ship around, but mentored and grew an unprecedented number of future commanding officers and senior sailors who continue to create additional leaders wherever they serve. His methods and lessons apply to every leadership challenge in military, business, or academia'

Rear Admiral Mark Kenny (USN, ret.), CEO, KENNCOR

'The best how-to manual anywhere for managers on delegating, training and driving flawless execution'

Fortune

Dedicated to the crew of the USS *Santa Fe*

CONTENTS

PART II

CONTROL
49

PART III

COMPETENCE
115

PART IV

CLARITY
161

ACKNOWLEDGMENTS

I'd like to acknowledge the crew of the USS *Santa Fe* who served with me from 1999 through 2001. They set aside their notions of what should be and engaged with me on a courageous journey. Whatever success I had was theirs.

Recognition goes to my publisher, Clint Greenleaf, who showed confidence in my project after a chance meeting in New York.

Admiral Hyman G. Rickover deserves credit for establishing the naval nuclear propulsion program. He interviewed me in 1981, selected me for the program, and gave me the opportunity to command a nuclear-powered submarine.

I'd like to acknowledge the inspirational leaders I've served with in the Navy including Marc Pelaez, Steve Howard, Mark Kenny, and Al Konetzni.

Great thanks go to my readers Dan Gillcrist, Jack Harrison, Lauren Kohl, and Rob Tullman, who immeasurably improved the document.

Special thanks go to Arthur Jacobson. His support sustained me during times when the project was in jeopardy of failing.

Stephen Covey rode *Santa Fe* in 2000 and played an enormously important role. Not only did his words in *7 Habits* show a path I hadn't seen, but his enthusiasm and faith in the project helped me maintain my resolve.

Simon Sinek played a key role as inspiration, mentor, critic, and coach. He has helped me find my Why. Thank you, Simon.

I would like to particularly acknowledge my wife, Jane, who gave me the courage to follow my own path and endured while I struggled to tell the story.

FOREWORD

I had the opportunity to ride the USS *Santa Fe* during Captain Marquet's command tour and observed firsthand the impact of his leadership approach. It had a profound impact on what I thought possible in terms of empowered and engaged workplaces.

I had been training U.S. Navy officers in leadership during the dot-com era when I started hearing about something really special happening on a submarine in Hawaii. When an opportunity arose to ride the *Santa Fe*, I jumped at it. I embarked on Captain Marquet's submarine to see what the buzz was about. Never before had I observed such empowerment. We stood on the bridge of this multibillion-dollar nuclear submarine in the crystal clear waters off Lahaina, Maui, moving silently along the surface of the water. Shortly after getting under way, a young officer approached the captain and said, "Sir, I intend to take this ship down four hundred feet." Captain Marquet asked about the sonar contacts and bottom depth and then instructed this young man to give us another few minutes on the bridge before carrying out his intention.

Throughout the day, people approached the captain intending to do this or to do that. The captain would sometimes ask a question or two, and then say, "Very well." He reserved only the tip-of-the-iceberg-type decisions for his own confirmation. The great mass of the iceberg—the other 95 percent of the decisions—were being made without any involvement or confirmation by the captain whatsoever. Wherever I went on the submarine—the control room, the torpedo room, even the galley where they were preparing lunch—I witnessed a dispersed intensity of operations I hadn't expected. The crew was amazingly involved and there was a constant low-level chatter of sharing information.

I can't say I actually saw the captain give an order.

I asked David how he achieved this turnabout. He said he wanted to empower his people as far as he possibly could within the Navy's confines, and maybe a little bit more. There was a mischievous twinkle in his eye when he told me that. He felt if he required them to own the problem and the solution to it, they would begin to view themselves as a vitally important link in the chain of command. He created a culture where those sailors had a real sense of adding value. But that answer only makes clear his objective, not what it actually takes—from the top man in the organization and everyone else—to accomplish this.

How do you create such an organization? What does it take?

The answer is in this book.

What I Love About This Book

First of all, this is a great story, one of self-discovery, tension, and the lonely self-doubts of the leader who sets off on an unknown path. We know now that Captain Marquet's experiment on the *Santa Fe* was wildly successful, but at the time, neither he nor the courageous crew who embraced this new way of running an organization knew if it would work.

Second, the book provides the specific mechanisms they used on the *Santa Fe* to achieve the transformation. We learn what they did, how the crew reacted—good or bad—and how the mechanisms matured with time. The good news is that these mechanisms are about how we interact as people, and are universally applicable. You can apply them in your organization—business, school, government, and family.

Third, the book presents a comprehensive paradigm shift for

how we think about leadership. Captain Marquet has coined the phrase "leader-leader" to differentiate it from the leader-follower approach that traditional leadership models have espoused. I think that laying out this distinction in such opposing terms is a good idea. Having personally witnessed how the *Santa Fe* operated, I can attest that this new way is not a nuanced modification of how we are doing business now; it is fundamentally different, and that is where its power lies.

Why You Want to Read This Book

No matter where you are in your company's organization chart, you'll want to read this book. People at the top will learn how they can release the passion, intellect, and energy of those below them. They may be unwittingly behaving and taking actions that work against those goals.

People on the front lines will also find ways to embrace decision making and make it easier for bosses to let go of control.

We are in the middle of one of the most profound shifts in human history, where the primary work of mankind is moving from the Industrial Age of "control" to the Knowledge Worker Age of "release." As Albert Einstein said, "The significant problems we face cannot be solved at the same level of thinking we were at when we created them." They certainly won't be solved by one person; even, and especially, the one "at the top."

Our world's bright future will be built by people who have discovered that leadership is the enabling art. It is the art of releasing human talent and potential. You may be able to "buy" a person's back with a paycheck, position, power, or fear, but a human being's genius, passion, loyalty, and tenacious creativity are *volunteered* only. The world's greatest problems will be solved by passionate, unleashed "volunteers."

My definition of leadership is this: Leadership is communicating to people their worth and potential so clearly that they are inspired to see it in themselves. I don't know of a finer model of this kind of empowering leadership than Captain Marquet's. And in the pages that follow, you will find a model for your pathway.

Remember, leadership is a choice, not a position. I wish you well on your voyage!

—STEPHEN R. COVEY, SPRING 2012

INTRODUCTION

People are frustrated.

Most of us are ready to give it our all when we start a job. We are usually full of ideas for ways to do things better. We eagerly offer our whole intellectual capacity only to be told that it's not our job, that it's been tried before, or that we shouldn't rock the boat. Initiative is viewed with skepticism. Our suggestions are ignored. We are told to follow instructions. Our work is reduced to following a set of prescriptions. Our creativity and innovations go unappreciated. Eventually, we stop trying and just toe the line. With resignation, we get by. Too often that's where the story of our work life ends.

Even the most promising employees can go through this downward evolutionary spiral. Take Ian, for example, who should have been viewed as a model employee by the multibillion-dollar communications company that hired him. Instead, his first corporate employment experience was so disheartening he swore never to return. He's now an entrepreneur. When I asked Ian what went wrong, he told me: "I could complete my day's work in two hours. I asked for more, and I was met with 'in time, young man.' I had no decision-making power." And this from a company that has a reputation for thoughtful leadership and innovative products!

Ian quit and found a more satisfying way to spend his time. "You know, sure, maybe over time things would have improved, but who wants to gamble their career—no, their life energy—on the hope of a sea change at an established, 'successful' company. I went on to pursue my dreams, and I've done so."

If you have felt the urge to follow Ian's example, you are not alone. Worker satisfaction in America is at an all-time low.[1] Worker engagement and commitment to their employers is also at a low.[2] As of November 2011, unemployment had been at 9 percent for thirty-one months. You'd think that everybody who had a job would be happy just to have one, but that is not the case.

This deliberate disengagement is costing billions in lost productivity. Disengaged, dissatisfied, uncommitted employees erode an organization's bottom line while breaking the spirits of their colleagues. Gallup estimates that within the U.S. workforce, this cost is more than $300 billion in lost productivity alone.[3] As large as the cost is in lost productivity, my sense is that it is dwarfed by the costs of lost joy and happiness.

Bosses are frustrated as well.

If you are a boss, you have likely been stymied by the lack of passion and ownership you see among your workforce. You probably have tried to encourage them to make decisions only to have many seem more comfortable simply doing what they are told. Empowerment programs start well but don't sustain themselves. New workers come into the organization straight from school expecting to be given prescriptions for how to do their work.

This situation exists in even the best companies. For example, Dr. Scott Mesh is CEO of Los Niños, a company dedicated to assisting with the educational development of special needs children. Los Niños has been a "Best Company to Work for in New York" award winner in multiple recent years. I met some of Scott's employees and recognized that he'd assembled a pretty elite team.

Still, Scott has his frustrations. "I'm babysitting too much. Some folks take care of stuff—they own it, grow it, love it, and have great results. Others need reminders—maybe they don't do the killer follow-up or they have other needs."

He is not alone. A recent survey indicated that 44 percent of business leaders reported their disappointment in the performance results of their employees.[4]

This vexation within both parties in the workplace has one root cause: our present leadership model, which is a painfully outdated one.

The Problem: Leader-Follower

When I served in the U.S. Navy, I had firsthand experience with an outdated leadership model. Here's what my Naval Academy leadership book told me about being a leader:

> Leadership is the art, science, or gift by which a person is enabled and privileged to direct the thoughts, plans, and actions of others in such a manner as to obtain and command their obedience, their confidence, their respect, and their loyal cooperation.[5]

In other words, leadership in the Navy, and in most organizations, is about controlling people. It divides the world into two groups of people: leaders and followers. Most of what we study, learn, and practice in terms of leadership today follows this leader-follower structure. This model has been with us for a long time. It is pervasive. It is the structure depicted in *The Iliad*, in *Beowulf*, and in other Western epics.

It permeates some of the most popular novels and movies about leadership, such as Patrick O'Brian's *Master and Commander*.

People can accomplish a tremendous amount through the leader-follower model, particularly with adept bosses. The widespread development of farming, the pyramids in Egypt, and the factories of the Industrial Revolution were all built using this structure. It generated tremendous wealth. Many bosses and owners got rich, and the followers were better off too. It is exactly because the leader-follower way of doing business has been so successful that it is both so appealing and so hard to give up. But this model developed during a period when mankind's primary work was physical. Consequently, it's optimized for extracting physical work from humans.

In our modern world, the most important work we do is cognitive; so, it's not surprising that a structure developed for physical work isn't optimal for intellectual work. People who are treated as followers have the expectations of followers and act like followers. As followers, they have limited decision-making authority and little incentive to give the utmost of their intellect, energy, and passion. Those who take orders usually run at half speed, under-utilizing their imagination and initiative. While this doesn't matter much for rowing a trireme, it's everything for operating a nuclear-powered submarine.

This is a recognized limitation of the leader-follower model.

We're taught the solution is empowerment.

The problem with empowerment programs is that they contain an inherent contradiction between the message and the method. While the message is "empowerment," the method—it takes me to empower you—fundamentally disempowers employees. That drowns out the message.

Additionally, in a leader-follower structure, the performance of the organization is closely linked to the ability of the leader. As a result, there is a natural tendency to develop personality-driven leadership. Followers gravitate toward the personality. Short-term performance is rewarded. When leaders who tend to do it all themselves and rely on personality depart, they are missed and performance can change significantly. Psychologically for the leader, this is tremendously rewarding. It is seductive. Psychologically for most followers, this is debilitating. The follower learns to rely on the leader to make all decisions rather than to fully engage with the work process to help make the organization run as efficiently as possible.

The Solution: Leader-Leader

The leader-leader structure is fundamentally different from the leader-follower structure. At its core is the belief that we can all be leaders and, in fact, it's best when we all are leaders. Leadership is not some mystical quality that some possess and others do not. As humans, we all have what it takes, and we all need to use our leadership abilities in every aspect of our work life.

The leader-leader model not only achieves great improvements in effectiveness and morale but also makes the organization stronger. Most critically, these improvements are enduring, decoupled from the leader's personality and presence. Leader-leader structures are significantly more resilient, and they do not rely on the designated leader always being right. Further, leader-leader structures spawn additional leaders throughout the organization naturally. It can't be stopped.

Born of Failure

When I reported to my first job as a junior officer on the USS *Sunfish* (SSN-649), a *Sturgeon*-class attack submarine, I was technically an expert on all the systems on the ship, including the intimate details of the reactor plant. I have always been an eager learner, and I graduated number one from my nuclear power school class and the submarine officer basic course. Between these advanced courses and my Naval Academy training I definitely knew a lot about submarines as well as leadership.

Technical expertise forms the basis of leadership in the nuclear Navy, and my first captain was an embodiment of that philosophy.

Brusque, aloof, but technically expert, he led *Sunfish* during our first, and highly successful, deployment. I didn't think twice about how he ran the ship—that was the way things were. Between my first and second deployments on *Sunfish*, we got a new captain, Commander (later Rear Admiral) Marc Pelaez. One day while we were cruising in the Atlantic Ocean during our training cycle and nothing much was going on, I saw a large merchant ship through the periscope. Sonar had been listening to it but they were not sure of its range because they had been authorized only for passive listening, the normal mode for submarines. I whimsically mused with the sonar chief how helpful it would be if they could ping on the merchant using active sonar, something we rarely did. Captain Pelaez appeared beside me. "Well, why don't you?" Of course he knew the reason—it takes the captain's permission to authorize going active on sonar. Sensing my discomfort, he said, "Why don't you just say, 'Captain, I intend to go active on sonar for training'?"

I tried it.

"Captain, I intend to go active on sonar for training."

He responded, "Very well." And disappeared, leaving me standing alone, and actually in charge for the first time.

For the next half hour, we pinged away using all the combinations of pulses we could with our sonar and cycling every sonarman through the sonar shack so they could see what an active surface contact looked like. The sonarmen loved using their equipment in novel ways. The sonar chief loved training his men. I loved it too. That taste of authority and ability to craft my watch team's training was a powerful tonic for me. I looked forward to my time on watch. When off watch, I spent hours studying and dreaming up new ways of training with my watch team.

After *Sunfish*, I served as a flag aide in the Pentagon and then went to the Naval Postgraduate School to get a year of Russian language training and a master's degree in national security affairs. After this respite, it was back to sea as the engineer (Eng) on board the USS *Will Rogers* (SSBN-659) from 1989 to 1991.

I thought I knew something about leadership. Turned out I didn't.

My tour on the *Will Rogers* was a disaster. We were in a dispiriting top-down leadership environment. No one wanted to be there. To change that, I intended to get the crew more involved and to decentralize decision making. I used all the tricks I had learned to "inspire and empower" my team, but none of those tricks seemed to improve either performance or morale. In fact, we ended up having a lot more problems. I just couldn't figure out what was going wrong. I felt like Ian and wanted to quit. After a while, I reverted to taking back the authority I had tried to share, micro-managing projects, and controlling every decision possible.

Eight years after departing *Will Rogers*, when I took command of the USS *Santa Fe* (SSN-763), one of the most modern nuclear-powered attack submarines (SSNs), that experience weighed heavily on me. The problems I encountered on *Santa Fe* reminded me of those I faced on *Will Rogers*. They were all fundamentally about people and leadership. I was resolved to try a new leadership approach.

Success, Immediately and Forever

A nuclear-powered submarine is an unlikely place for a leadership revolution to occur. It operates in an unforgiving environment. Deadlines are tight, as is space. When no one is ever farther than 150 feet away from the control room, it's easy to adopt a highly hierarchical management structure. Naval tradition and the approach of the naval nuclear power program, which stresses accountability and technical competence, reinforce that natural accretion of power, authority, and control at the top. Submarines, which can operate for extended periods without radio communication, are the closest things we have to the far-ranging frigates of old. In short, they offer the perfect environment for reinforcing leader-follower.

When I took command of *Santa Fe*, its crew were at the bottom of the fleet—technically, operationally, and emotionally.

Within a year, the situation was totally turned around. We went from worst to first in most measures of performance, including the one I valued most—our ability to retain our sailors and officers. The steps were evolutionary. The result was revolutionary.

Santa Fe performed superbly while I served as its captain. If that had been it, this would be the same personality-driven leadership story that occupies so much space on bookshelves now. Only ten years later can we assess the true success of that work—with *Santa Fe*'s continued operational excellence and the implausibly high promotion rates for its officers and crew. This is the legacy of leader-leader.

Turn the Ship Around! is the story of that journey and the men aboard *Santa Fe* who lived it with me. It describes essentially four phases in my struggle to change the way we interacted for the better. I describe how I needed to let go of old ideas to make room for new ones in Part I. In Parts II, III, and IV, I describe the bridge to leader-leader and supporting pillars. The bridge is control, divesting control to others in your organization while keeping responsibility. Control, we discovered, only works with a competent workforce that understands the organization's purpose. Hence, as control is divested, both technical competence and organizational clarity need to be strengthened. The book parts are generally grouped into these categories, but the reality of how this works is that these cycles are repeated in ever increasing circles.

I imagine a world where we all find satisfaction in our work. It is a world where every human being is intellectually engaged, motivated, and self-inspired. Our cognitive capacity as a race is fully engaged in solving the monumental problems that we face.

Ultimately, this book is a call to action, a manifesto, for all those frustrated workers and bosses for whom the current leadership structure just isn't working. We need to reject leader-follower as a model and view the world as a place for leaders everywhere to achieve this vision. Whether you are a boss, an employee, a teacher, or a parent, you will find ways to work toward this goal.

Have fun, and let me know how leader-leader works for you. Send me your stories and thoughts at david@turntheshiparound .com.

CAST OF CHARACTERS

CAPTAIN MARK KENNY

Prospective Commanding Officer (PCO) instructor and later Commodore, Submarine Squadron Seven, to which USS *Santa Fe* was assigned.

LIEUTENANT COMMANDER TOM STANLEY

Executive officer (XO) on *Santa Fe* 1999–2000.

LIEUTENANT COMMANDER MIKE BERNACCHI

XO on *Santa Fe* 2000–2.

LIEUTENANT COMMANDER RICK PANLILIO

Engineer (Eng) on *Santa Fe* 1998–2001.

LIEUTENANT COMMANDER BILL GREENE

Navigator (Nav) on *Santa Fe* 1997–99.

LIEUTENANT DAVE ADAMS

Weapons officer (Weps) on *Santa Fe* 1998–2001.

LIEUTENANT CALEB KERR

Nav on *Santa Fe* 2000–4.

SENIOR CHIEF ANDY WORSHEK

Chief Sonarman and Weapons Department Chief on *Santa Fe* 1998–2002.

CHIEF DAVID STEELE

Chief Fire Controlman on *Santa Fe* 1996–2000.

CHIEF BRAD JENSEN

Senior Nuclear Chief (bull nuke) on *Santa Fe* 1998–2000.

CHIEF MIKE CIKO

Senior Nuclear Chief (bull nuke) on *Santa Fe* 2000–2.

YN2 SCOTT DILLON

Yeoman Division Leader on *Santa Fe* 1998–2001.

SLED DOG

Quartermaster (Navigation Plotter) on *Santa Fe* 1998–2001.

PART I

STARTING OVER

Our greatest struggle is within ourselves. Whatever sense we have of thinking we know something is a barrier to continued learning. For me, my ideas of leadership were formed by reading Western classics like *Beowulf* and *The Odyssey*, reading histories of the sea, and watching popular movies. These notions of "leader as individual hero" were strongly reinforced when I got to the U.S. Naval Academy.

In this part of the book, I describe my frustration, questioning, and ultimate rejection of that type of leadership. I didn't realize it at the time, but the assumption behind that leadership structure, so fundamental that it becomes subconscious, is that there are leaders and there are followers. It was only after I cleared my mind of these preconceptions that I was able to see a truly better way for humans to interact.

Pain

How has failure shaped you? As a department head, I tried to implement a new leadership approach on *Will Rogers* and failed.

1989: The Irish Sea

Eight thousand tons of steel moved silently, hidden in the depths of the Irish Sea. In the control room of the USS *Will Rogers* (SSBN-659), the officer of the deck (OOD) ordered the ship toward the deeper, wider expanses of the North Atlantic. Glancing at the missile control panel, he could see the status of the sixteen Poseidon missiles on board, each capable of carrying fourteen multiple nuclear-armed reentry vehicles. These missiles were the sole reason for the existence of the *Will Rogers*, a nuclear-powered ballistic missile submarine—SSBN for short—the kind of submarine the crew affectionately called a "boomer." One thing above all else mattered for a boomer: to be at sea and in a condition that would enable it to execute a strike if so ordered. SSBNs were a vital component of America's strategic deterrence.

The control room was the nerve center of the ship. So important were its sixteen missiles, invulnerable to attack once under way and submerged, that boomers had two crews—a Blue Crew and a Gold Crew—to maximize the time the submarine could spend at sea on strategic deterrent patrol. The crews lived near New London, Connecticut, and *Will Rogers* was operated out of a forward base at Holy Loch, Scotland. Every three months the crews would swap, with a three-day turnover period. After assuming the boat from the other crew, the new crew would spend four weeks doing the necessary corrective and preventive maintenance before going to sea. In order for the United States to have a credible strategic deterrent, the missiles needed to be ready to go. If *Will Rogers* couldn't make it on time another submarine would have to remain at sea longer.

Forty-one of these ballistic missile submarines were built between 1958 and 1965 in response to the Soviet threat, an impressive industrial accomplishment. *Will Rogers* was the last of the forty-one SSBNs and had operated nearly continuously since its commissioning. Those original submarines were being replaced by the newer and more capable *Ohio* class; however, *Will Rogers* still had important operational tasking to perform. Nevertheless, after thirty-three years, it was a tired ship. Worse, during the patrol before I reported aboard, *Will Rogers* had collided with a trawler and failed an important certification.

I checked the chart in the control room. We were on track to start the deep dive in about half an hour. I walked aft, past the rows of missile tubes and the reactor compartment to the engine room. With my flashlight, I started doing a last-minute walkabout. All our repairs had been properly certified as completed but it wouldn't hurt to do one more visual check.

As engineer officer for the Blue Crew, I was responsible for inspecting the nuclear reactor and important auxiliary equipment and supervising the sixty men who maintained and operated it. There was a constant tension between doing things right and meeting deadlines; every member of the crew felt it. The job was grueling and I wasn't particularly happy with how things were going.

The officer I relieved was very involved in details. He was always reviewing technical documents and directing maintenance and other operations. I was determined to change that— by giving the men more control of their work, more decision-making authority, and fewer lists of tasks. In doing so, I hoped to bring the passion I'd experienced on *Sunfish* to *Will Rogers*. In this, I was going against the tide.

Just prior to going aboard, I'd had the chance to ride another SSBN for several days. It was undergoing an underway warfighting inspection, and the crew were tasked with different missions that required significant internal coordination. I followed the captain around to see what he did. He was everywhere: dashing to the engine room, then back to control; running to sonar and from there to the torpedo room. I was exhausted before twenty-four hours were over. I'm not sure he ever slept during the three days I was observing.

That ship did well on its inspection, and the inspection team specifically cited the involvement of the captain. I had a sense of unease because I knew that wasn't how I wanted to run a submarine. Even if it were, I knew I could not physically do what he did.

Even though the Navy encouraged this kind of top-down leadership, I pressed forward with my *Sunfish*-inspired plan to give control to the department rather than orders. For example, rather than giving specific lists of tasks to the division officers and chiefs of the *Will Rogers*, I gave broad guidance and told them to prepare the task lists and present the lists to me. Rather than telling everyone what we needed to do, I would ask questions about how they thought we should approach a problem. Rather than being the central hub coordinating maintenance between two divisions, I told the division chiefs to talk to each other directly.

Things did not go well. During the maintenance period, we made several errors that required us to redo work. We fell behind schedule. We also had several jobs that didn't start on time because the mid-level management had not assembled all the parts and permissions, or established the propulsion plant conditions necessary to do the work. I overheard people wishing for the old engineer back, who would just "tell them what to do." Indeed, it would have been much faster just to tell people what to do, and I frequently found myself barking out a list of orders just to get the work done. I wasn't happy with myself, but no one else seemed to mind much. I seemed to be the only one who wanted a more democratic and empowered workplace, and I wondered if I was on the right track.

It was touch and go, but as the maintenance period came to an end, my efforts to empower others seemed to be working. There was a budding sense of optimism; we'd make it on time.

In a moment, I realized we wouldn't.

I dropped down the ladder into the lower level of the engine room. I was scanning the various pieces of equipment with my flashlight when I was stopped cold by what I saw. The nuts holding the bolts for the end bell of a large seawater heat exchanger had been improperly installed. The nuts weren't sufficiently grabbing the threads on the bolt. They were close, but I was sure they didn't meet the technical specification. Someone had taken a shortcut. This cooler was subjected to full submergence pressure. Even a small leak would cause seawater to spray into the ship with tremendous force. Failure would be catastrophic.

My heart sank. The deep dive should be starting shortly. I needed to cancel that immediately. Not only would we need to reassemble this cooler; we would need to inspect all the other coolers to make sure the mistake hadn't been repeated. Most important of all, we would need to figure out how this had happened.

I called the OOD and told him we'd need to postpone the deep dive. Then I started the long walk forward to tell the captain. Walking past the sixteen tubes in the missile compartment, I felt quite alone. The reputation of the ship and my department would suffer. My efforts at empowering my team had failed. This should never have happened. As expected, the captain had a fit. Of course, that didn't help fix the problem.

After this, things got worse. I had wanted to give my team more authority and control, but my heart wasn't in it anymore. I would give decision-making control to my people, but they'd make bad decisions. If I was going to get yelled at, I at least wanted it to be my fault. I went back to leading in the way I'd been taught. I personally briefed every event. I approved all decisions myself. I set up systems where reports came to me all day and all night. I never slept well because messengers were waking me so I could make decisions. I was exhausted and miserable; the men in the department weren't happy either, but they stoically went about their jobs. I prevented any more major problems, but everything hinged on me. Numerous times I found errors. Far from being proud of catching these mistakes, I lamented my indispensability and worried what would happen when I was tired, asleep, or wrong.

I assessed my chances of being selected for executive officer, my next career milestone, as low. None of the other department heads on the *Will Rogers* were selected (screened) for executive officer. None of the department heads on the Gold Crew screened either. Neither executive officer screened for captain. The captain wasn't promoted. The *Will Rogers* was a cemetery for careers. I made plans to do something else with my life. I took a job doing START and INF treaty inspections in the former Soviet Union with the On-Site Inspection Agency instead of going to a submarine staff job.

I returned from an inspection in Volgograd to find a message in my inbox. I had screened for executive officer, the next step after my tour as the engineering department head—I would be going back to sea on a submarine. I should have been ecstatic. Executive officer was one step below captain. Instead, I was strangely ambivalent. I would have to grapple with the tension between how I aspired to be as a leader and how I actually was.

Thinking Anew

While assigned to the On-Site Inspection Agency I had to contemplate what had happened on the *Will Rogers*. I started reading everything I could about leadership, management, psychology, communication, motivation, and human behavior. I thought deeply about what motivated me and how I wanted to be treated.

I remembered the release of energy, passion, and creativity I had experienced running my own watch team on the *Sunfish*. I was motivated to avoid any reoccurrence of the pain, frustration, and emptiness of my three years on the *Will Rogers*, both being directed and directing others.

At the end of that study, I was troubled by three contradictions.

First, though I liked the idea of empowerment, I didn't understand why empowerment was needed. It seemed to me that humans are born in a state of action and natural empowerment. After all, it wasn't likely that a species that was naturally passive could have taken over the planet. Empowerment programs appeared to be a reaction to the fact that we had actively disempowered people. Additionally, it seemed inherently contradictory to have an empowerment program whereby I would empower my subordinates and my boss would empower me. I felt my power came from within, and attempts to empower me felt like manipulation.

Second, the way I was told to manage others was not the way I wanted to be managed. I felt I was at my best when given specific goals but broad latitude in how to accomplish them. I didn't respond well to executing a bunch of tasks. In fact, being treated that way irritated me and caused me to shut my brain down. That was intellectually wasteful and unfulfilling.

Third, I was disturbed by the close coupling of the technical competence of the leader with the performance of the organization. Ships with a "good" commanding officer (CO) did well, as had the SSBN I rode. Ships that didn't have a good CO didn't do well. But a good ship could become a bad ship overnight when a new CO came aboard. And there was a further twist: every so often a mishap occurred that caused people to shake their heads and lament, "It happened on such a good ship." It seems the captain had made a mistake, and the crew, lemming-like, just followed him. I concluded that competence could not rest solely with the leader. It had to run throughout the entire organization.

Essentially, what I had been trying to achieve on *Will Rogers* was to run an empowerment program within a leader-follower structure. The leadership structure, which was strongly reinforced by the behavior and expectations of the captain, was one of "Do what you are told." Hence, my efforts amounted to little more than "Do what you are told, but . . ." It just didn't work.

What I was trying to do was an extension of the way things worked on *Sunfish*. On that ship, I was empowered, but the sense of leadership stopped with me. Those in my watch team were followers in the traditional model. What made it so liberating was that for those six hours, I didn't feel like a follower. That's what I had wanted to pass on to the officers and crew of the *Will Rogers* engineering department.

One of the things that limits our learning is our belief that we already know something. My experience on the *Will Rogers* convinced me there was something fundamentally wrong with our approach. Simply exhorting people to be proactive, take ownership, be involved, and all the other aspects of an empowerment program just scratched the surface. It was only after serving on the *Will Rogers* that I opened myself up to new ideas about leadership. I began to seriously question the image of the sea captain as "master and commander." I began to wonder whether everything I'd been taught about leadership was wrong.

QUESTIONS TO CONSIDER

- Why do we need empowerment?
- Do you need someone else to empower you?
- How reliant is your organization on the decision making of one person, or a small group of people?
- What kind of leadership model does your business or organization use?
- When you think of movie images that depict leadership, who/what comes to mind?
- What assumptions are embedded in those images?
- How do these images influence how you think about yourself as a leader?
- To what extent do these images limit your growth as a leader?

Business as Usual

Are you and your people working to optimize the organization for their tenure, or forever? To promote long-term success, I had to ignore the short-term reward systems.

December 1998: Pearl Harbor, Hawaii

The USS *Olympia* (SSN-717) was heading out the main Pearl Harbor channel *without me*. I hadn't expected that.

I'd been training for twelve months to take command of this specific submarine, and my change of command was in less than four weeks. It was a dream assignment. *Olympia* was a frontline SSN (a nuclear-powered attack submarine)—exactly what I'd hoped for. While *Will Rogers*'s mission was to hide in the vastness of the ocean, attack boats were the hunters and would take the fight to the enemy. I had studied the equipment configuration and piping diagrams, the exact reactor plant, the schedule, the weapons, and every problem report the ship had issued in the previous three years. I learned the career status of each officer and read his biography. I reviewed every inspection report: tactical inspections, reactor inspections, safety inspections, food service inspections. For a year, I'd been doing nothing but think about the sailors on *Olympia* and my responsibility to lead them for the next three years. In the way of the nuclear Navy, I had gained an intimate technical knowledge of the ship. I had loved the prospective commanding officer (PCO) training I had just completed. As a student, I was responsible only for myself for an entire year! In addition to the specifics of *Olympia*, we learned tactics and leadership. I attended a weeklong leadership school in Newport, Rhode Island, and my wife Jane had been able to join me. The entire training course culminated with an intense two-week period at sea driving submarines hard and shooting torpedoes.

The officers leading PCO training were hand-selected from among proven captains; Captain Mark Kenny, who had commanded the *Los Angeles*–class submarine USS *Birmingham* (SSN-698), led my group. Mark inspired us to great learning as well as introspection. Every day we learned about our submarines, and ourselves.

During one torpedo approach, I devised an elaborate ruse that would flush out the opposing submarine and make it a sitting duck for our attack. I predicted to the officers in the control room—in this case, other PCOs—what would happen. The situation developed exactly as I'd foreseen, and we were able to get a hit on a quiet and tenacious enemy. In the middle of the attack, however, I'd had to reach over and do the job of one of the other PCOs because he had gotten confused.

I thought I was brilliant, but Captain Kenny took me aside and upbraided me. It didn't matter how smart my plan was if the team couldn't execute it! It was a lesson that would serve me well.

Olympia was doing well. Its retention numbers were good and its inspection scores were above average. Operationally, it had a reputation on the waterfront for getting it done—that is, fulfilling the missions assigned to it. I wondered what kind of a leadership approach I'd want to apply aboard *Olympia*.

I was keen to get aboard this workhorse of the fleet and finish the turnover process. During the month I was to spend on board before taking command, the ship would be in port for a maintenance period except for this two-day evaluation of the ship's ability to operate the reactor plant. Accordingly, I arranged to ride with the inspection team to meet the *Olympia* at the entrance to Pearl Harbor.

This would not only be my only opportunity to see the ship and crew operate at sea before taking command, it would also be tremendously useful for me to watch the ship go through the inspection. I would be without the emotional attachment of being part of the crew, but I would be responsible for carrying out any corrective action after I took over.

As *Olympia* appeared in the channel and approached the turning basin, the radios crackled on the small boat. The coxswain reported the passengers he expected to transfer to "Oly." And then word came back from the *Olympia*: only the inspection team would come aboard, *not* the PCO. I wasn't allowed on board. I "must have misunderstood" the plan. I watched as the submarine turned around and the small boat came alongside, put the brow across, and transferred the inspection team to Oly. I could see the captain on the bridge but we never made eye contact. Then the brow was raised and Oly returned to sea. The small boat carried me back to the inner harbor and dropped me off.

I was miffed that the captain didn't want me aboard. He was depriving me of seeing the boat operate and watching the inspection. In less than a month, I was going to be totally accountable for the performance of this submarine but wouldn't be able to see it under way.

Yet, at one level, who could blame him? I would take up another bunk and inconvenience a crew member. Even though this two-day underway period at sea would be greatly useful in sustaining *Olympia*'s quality performance after he departed, he apparently had no interest in helping facilitate that. Could I fault him? In the Navy system, captains are graded on how well their ships perform up to the day they depart; not a day longer. After that it becomes someone else's problem.

I thought about that. On every submarine and ship, and in every squadron and battalion, hundreds of captains were making thousands of decisions to optimize the performance of their commands for their tour and their tour alone. If they did anything for the long run it was because of an enlightened sense of duty, not because there was anything in the system that rewarded them for it. We didn't associate an officer's leadership effectiveness with how well his unit performed after he left. We didn't associate an officer's leadership effectiveness with how often his people got promoted two, three, or four years hence. We didn't even track that kind of information. All that mattered was performance in the moment.

Nothing to See Here, Move Along

I did get aboard *Olympia*—three days later, when it was tied to the pier. As expected, it had done well on its inspection.

My turnover on *Olympia* was straightforward: a review of the records, material inspections, and interviews with the officers and crew. As I walked about the ship, I noted that the crew seemed alert and confident. Almost *too* confident, actually. Because I had a detailed knowledge of the ship, the systems, and the trouble reports, I was able to pinpoint technical issues I wanted to explore. I asked lots of questions about why we did things certain ways. The crew's answers were concise and certain. I soon realized there wasn't any impetus for change. Oly was operating in a top-down, business-as-usual structure, and everyone liked it that way.

I thought about how I would lead the ship when I took over. I shelved my ideas for a radical management change because there would be too much internal resistance. The crew, doing well, wouldn't see the need. I was resigned to executing incremental changes on the standard hierarchical structure.

It is precisely the success of the top-down, leader-follower structure that makes it so appealing. As long as you are measuring performance over just the short run, it can be effective. Officers are rewarded for being indispensable, for being missed after they depart. When the performance of a unit goes down after an officer leaves, it is taken as a sign that he was a good leader, not that he was ineffective in training his people properly.

Another factor that makes this leadership approach appealing is the induced numbness. It absolves subordinates of the hard work of thinking, making decisions, and being responsible and accountable. You are just a cog, an executor of the decisions of others. "Hey, I was only doing what I was told." People get comfortable with this.

There's a cost to the people, though, which only becomes evident over time. People who are treated as followers treat others as followers when it's their turn to lead. A vast untapped human potential is lost as a result of treating people as followers. Only in the long run—three to ten years later—does it become obvious, but by that time people have moved on to new jobs.

With *Olympia* sitting pierside I sped through my program reviews, inspections, and interviews. Already a technical expert on the ship, I got bored with the turnover and decided to take a week's vacation with my wife. There was a venerable cruise ship, the SS *Independence*, that cruised around the Hawaiian Islands, and we decided to spend the last week before the change of command on a cruise. The first four days were pretty relaxing, observing the beauty of the islands. I was comfortable with how Oly was operating, and the leadership was going to be right up my alley— the same kind that had gotten me through *Will Rogers*.

On the fifth morning, while our cruise ship was passing the lava flowing into the ocean from Kilauea, I received a phone call.

In those days it was unusual to receive a call from shore and I assumed it was an internal call. I was startled to hear a crackly voice on the other end inform me that my change of command was canceled. I would be taking over the *Santa Fe* instead, just after New Year's.

I was panicked. The foundation of my leadership approach, my technical competence, was for the wrong submarine.

QUESTIONS TO CONSIDER

- In your organization, are people rewarded for what happens after they transfer?
- Are they rewarded for the success of their people?
- Do people want to be "missed" after they leave?
- When an organization does worse immediately after the departure of a leader, what does this say about that person's leadership? How does the organization view this situation?
- How does the perspective of time horizon affect our leadership actions?
- What can we do to incentivize long-term thinking?

Change of Course

What's your level of commitment? I discovered that the hardest thing about my planned turnaround project was my own fortitude.

December 1998: Pearl Harbor, Hawaii

The first thing I did when we returned from our cruise was to visit my new boss and former PCO instructor, Commodore Mark Kenny. Instead of heading down to the submarine piers to continue my turnover on *Olympia*, I veered into the building that had housed the Pacific Fleet commander's office during the December 7, 1941, attack on Pearl Harbor. Now the Navy's three Pearl Harbor squadron commanders have their offices in that building. I was literally taking a new turn. The *Olympia* was in Squadron Three and *Santa Fe* was in Squadron Seven. My mentor from PCO training, Commodore Mark Kenny, had just taken over Squadron Seven so he was going to be my new boss. Mark had argued forcefully for me to be assigned the job of turning *Santa Fe* around. He had credibility because he'd be living with his recommendation. It was the reason I got the job.

Later Mark told me that one of the reasons he argued for me was that I'd evinced a particular enthusiasm for learning throughout the entire PCO course. He sensed that a keen curiosity would be vital for the successful about-face of *Santa Fe* and its crew, a fact I would later deeply appreciate in ways I didn't then imagine.

When I got the news that I would be taking command of *Santa Fe*, it was a shock. I didn't know much about *Santa Fe* other than it was stationed in Pearl Harbor and scheduled to deploy in six months. In contrast to the *Olympia*, *Santa Fe* was the ship we all joked about during the PCO training pipeline. A damning photograph of *Santa Fe*'s inattentive crewmen had been released on the Internet the previous year. It earned the captain a scolding and was used as a training example of how not to be. *Santa Fe* was the ship that had trouble getting under way on time. And *Santa Fe* had the worst retention in the submarine force: in 1998, for example, it reenlisted only three crew members.

Mark discussed my new job. "You need to get *Santa Fe* and your crew ready for deployment in six months. It's a dream deployment from an operational perspective, with the *Constellation* Battle Group, but it's also going to be demanding. One of the things we're going to try and set up is a torpedo exercise in the shallow Arabian Gulf, to demonstrate our combat effectiveness."

What Mark said next didn't present a pretty sight. "I'm not going to minimize the task in front of you. The ship isn't doing well. It looks from here like there's a leadership vacuum. This is a unique situation. In all my time on the waterfront, I can't remember such a particular confluence of events.

"Look, here's the deal. If you need to change out some people, let me know, but I'm not interested in a lot of turnover. I don't think that will help the crew. I think a better focus would be on working with what you've got. With only six months to deployment you don't have a lot of time to find replacements."

I was thinking that too. In the end, I fired no one.

This was important because it sent the message to each crew member that he wasn't screwed up, the leadership was. My challenge would be to use the same people and support team and by changing the way they interacted and behaved, dramatically increase the combat effectiveness of *Santa Fe*.

As the captain, I would be assisted by an executive officer (XO), the second in command, who was qualified to take command in case I became incapacitated. There would be the four department heads: weapons, engineering, navigation/operations, and supply. Each department head except the supply officer (Suppo) would be trained in nuclear power and could aspire to command his own submarine someday. The odds were, however, that only one of the three officers would. The jury was out on these men. Mark explained that the XO seemed to be closely identified with the outgoing captain, and two of the department heads were too new to assess.

"Look, you've got one hundred percent from me and my squadron staff," Mark continued, "to help you get the ship ready. We aren't going to walk down there and tell you what you need, but whatever you think you need, we'll support."

We also talked about the junior officers. As a group, they were ignored, untrained, and not staying in the Navy. Because this was their first tour, these men were probably the most neglected group on board. All they'd known about submarining and how to be an officer, other than academically, was based on *Santa Fe*. They were a mix: about half had graduated from the Naval Academy, and about half came out of NROTC.

We talked about *Santa Fe* chiefs. Unempowered, uninspired. The twelve chiefs are the senior enlisted men. They are middle management. At our submarine schools, the instructors tell us that officers make sure we do the right things and chiefs make sure we do things right. Their technical expertise and leadership would be key, as would my ability to tap their expertise.

Just as underway time on patrol was the reason the nation built SSBNs, deployments were the reason the nation built SSNs.

Deployments were a period of operating for six months away from home port.

During that time, we'd be mostly submerged, operating in areas where our potential adversaries might operate. We'd surface and make port calls to resupply and conduct minor repairs, but overall, we'd need to travel thirty thousand miles on our own. Submarines were most useful forward, in hostile waters, and not sitting back under the protection of the carrier battle group or other allied forces. Deployments required the ship and crew to be at peak maintenance, training, manning, and supply conditions.

The commodore explained that there weren't going to be any breaks in the schedule to accommodate the abrupt change in captain. The Navy and nation needed *Santa Fe* to be a "full-up round"—that is, a fully capable submarine. Mark would have the final say on whether my submarine was ready to deploy. His parting words of encouragement: "I have great confidence in your ability to do this. And just one piece of advice, you might want to get a good flashlight."

We shook hands and I headed down to the boat. How were we—how was *I*—going to do this? I wasn't sure it was a possible task. I felt overwhelmed and didn't know where to start. Preparing for deployment was daunting enough, let alone with a demoralized crew. Was I willing to risk implementing a new leadership approach as well?

Upon reflection, Commodore Kenny was providing great leadership. He presented me with a specific goal—have *Santa Fe* ready for deployment in every way—but did not tell me how to do it. The other thing he was telling me was that the people and resources available to the ship would be the same as they were before and the same as they were to any other submarine. Consequently, the only thing we could change was how we acted and interacted. This would be my focus.

Then I began to reconsider the situation. Since Mark wasn't

going to micromanage me, maybe *this* was a chance to do something different. Maybe this was the chance to set the crew free from the top-down, "do what you're told" approach to leadership. Maybe this was the opportunity of a lifetime. Of course, I would be solely responsible, and if *Santa Fe* wasn't ready, it would be my fault and likely my job.

I resolved to give it a try. I left his office and headed down to the pier where *Santa Fe* was berthed.

QUESTIONS TO CONSIDER

- What are you willing to personally risk? (Sometimes taking a step for the better requires caring/not caring. Caring deeply about the people and mission, but not caring about the bureaucratic consequences to your personal career.)
- What must leaders overcome mentally and emotionally to give up control yet retain full responsibility?
- What's the hardest thing you experience in letting go of micromanaging, top-down leadership, or the cult of personality?
- How can you get your project teams interacting differently but still use the same resources?
- What can you as a subordinate do to get your boss to let you try a new way of handling a project?
- Do you give employees specific goals as well as the freedom to meet them in any way they choose?

Frustration

Are you curious? I thought I was being curious during my previous tours; turns out I was only "questioning."

December 15, 1998: On Board USS *Santa Fe*, Pearl Harbor, Hawaii
(twenty-five days to change of command)

I approached *Santa Fe* with a mix of curiosity and anxiety.

In the U.S. Navy, we name the submarine classes after the hull number of the first ship in the class. The *Los Angeles*–class submarines are 688s, and the class was split into two "flights": first flight and second flight. The *Olympia* is the thirtieth ship of the first flight 688s; *Santa Fe* is a second-flight 688. Other than the overall hull shape, the ships are significantly different. The first-flight 688s have sail planes, four torpedo tubes, and a reactor plant that needs to be refueled once during the life of the ship. The second-flight 688s have bow planes, twelve vertical-launch Tomahawk land-attack missile (TLAM) tubes in addition to the four torpedo tubes, and a redesigned reactor plant that has enough fuel to last the entire life of the ship.

I descended the narrow hatch. As I passed through the mess decks, I heard the topside watch announcing "Commander, United States Navy, arriving" per protocol. I made my way forward through the narrow passageways. I pleasantly greeted each crew member I passed. The passageways in a submarine are about two feet wide; you can't pass someone without acknowledging their presence. It's just like passing someone in the aisle of an airplane. Mostly I got mumbles or grunts and a lot of men looking down at their shoes. They seemed embarrassed. They avoided eye contact. They avoided conversing. These guys were beaten. They had been told over and over they were the worst ship in the submarine force and they believed it. Just across the water from *Olympia*, it was worlds away.

I stopped by the captain's stateroom to let him know I was on board. I was his relief, and in a couple weeks this would be my responsibility; but right now it was his. That was a bit awkward since he would be leaving command a year early. Eventually I would be assigned the second desk in the XO's stateroom for my base of operations, but for the moment I didn't have a place. The change in orders had caught the crew of *Santa Fe* by surprise too. Not having a place to plop down, I walked into the control room and looked around instead. The equipment was shut down but I could see from the panel faces, gauges, and dials that it was different from what I'd seen before. Since I didn't have a place I started wandering around the ship. After a time I started asking nearby crew members about the various pieces of equipment. For the first time, I was truly curious.

Walking the ship, I would ask the crew questions about their equipment and what they were working on. They were skeptical about these questions initially. That's because normally I would have been "questioning," not curious. I would have been asking questions to make sure they knew the equipment. Now I was asking questions to make sure I knew the equipment.

My unfamiliarity with the sub's technical details was having an interesting side effect: since I couldn't get involved with the specifics of the gear, I opened up space to focus on the people and their interactions instead, and to rely on the crew more than I normally would have. I decided I'd do physical inspections of the ship and review the records, but only as a guise for understanding the crew. Whereas on Oly I had reviewed some records by myself, I decided that everything I did on *Santa Fe* would be with an officer, a chief, or a crew member.

I started interviewing the chiefs and officers in their spaces. After having them tell me about their people, I asked them a loosely structured set of questions like these:

- What are the things you are hoping I don't change?
- What are the things you secretly hope I do change?
- What are the good things about *Santa Fe* we should build on?
- If you were me what would you do first?
- Why isn't the ship doing better?
- What are your personal goals for your tour here on *Santa Fe*?
- What impediments do you have to doing your job?
- What will be our biggest challenge to getting *Santa Fe* ready for *deployment*?
- What are your biggest frustrations about how *Santa Fe* is currently *run*?
- What is the best thing I can do for you?

Later, I thought about some of the things I had heard. A lot of things were problems with how *Santa Fe* did business.

- "Admin disappears into a black hole."
- "The duty officers delay getting maintenance started."
- "The junior officers are the source of low standards."

- "I was previously qualified for this watch station, transferred ship to ship, and now have to start over with a blank qualification card."
- "I've been waiting for four weeks to get a test so that I can qualify."
- "There's no participation in the wives' club."
- "The radio installation and upgrade we just received left us with less capability than what we had before."
- "I was promised a certain job when I came here, and it hasn't happened."
- "I just keep my head down and try to stay out of trouble. When things go badly, I secretly hope someone else will screw up next."

The conversation I had with Fire Control Technician (FT) Chief David Steele was typical. "I've asked to be transferred," he admitted. Chief Steele had been on board *Santa Fe* for two years and wasn't having fun. He wasn't one of the command's favorites and wasn't moving up in the performance rankings. A high school dropout, Steele had gone to see the Navy recruiter when he turned eighteen. He performed well enough on the aptitude test to be selected for submarines, so the recruiter convinced him to take the GED and enlist. Now, Steele ran the fire control system (FCS) that sent targeting instructions to every missile and torpedo *Santa Fe* launched.

"I still haven't even signed my evaluation," he told me. I resisted the urge to comment on what a disservice this was to him. December already, and evaluations were due on September 15. His file would be incomplete when the promotion board met, reducing his chances to zero. I wondered, if the chiefs' evaluations are this bad, what about the junior enlisted men?

"And I don't like how the command is handling evals, anyway," Chief Steele grumbled.

His "tell it like it is" style may have grated on some, but I appreciated it. He was key to the *Santa Fe*'s combat effectiveness, and his knowledge of the vertical launch missile system (VLS) was especially important for me.

"Look, Chief, I can't promise I'll make you an EP, but I can promise that performance rankings are going to be based on your contribution to the ship's mission, period." (EP is the highest competitive ranking—it stands for "early promote.")

On another occasion, the chief responsible for a nuclear division told me, "No one has reviewed my equipment status log [ESL] since I've been here." The ESL is a large database that includes details about everything that's wrong with each piece of equipment the division owns and therefore forms the basis of the maintenance and operational plans.

I was uneasy not being the technical expert on each and every piece of equipment on board. The impact of this focus on people was that I was going to have to rely on the crew to provide me with the technical details about how the submarine worked. This went against every grain of my naval leadership and scientific training. But the circumstances demanded a new mode of operation. Doing the same thing as everyone else and hoping for a different outcome didn't make sense.

I am not advocating being ignorant about the equipment. For me, however, it was a necessary step to make me truly curious and reliant upon the crew in a way I wouldn't have been without it. Later in my tour I became a technical expert on all aspects of *Santa Fe*, but the positive patterns had been set and I continued in the same relationship with the crew. If you walk about your organization talking to people, I'd suggest that you be as curious as possible. As with a good dinner table conversationalist, one question should naturally lead to another. The time to be questioning or even critical is after trust has been established.

QUESTIONS TO CONSIDER

Are you asking questions to make sure *you* know or to make sure *they* know?

- Do you have to be the smartest person in your organization?
- To what degree does technical competence form the basis for leadership?
- Is that technical competence a personal competence or an organizational competence?
- How do you know what is going on "at the deck plate" in your organization?

Call to Action

When was the last time you walked around your organization to hear about the good, the bad, and the ugly of top-down management? Walking around and listening was my first step in preparing to command *Santa Fe*.

December 16, 1998: On Board USS *Santa Fe*, Pearl Harbor, Hawaii (twenty-four days to change of command)

According to procedure, I was to spend the next two weeks reviewing everything on the ship, including training records, school records, administrative records, award records, advancement records, records pertaining to the operation and maintenance of the reactor plant, the weapons system, the torpedoes and missiles, schedules, exercises, classified material, and so on. I ignored that. Instead, I spent my time walking around the ship talking to people. I also set up a series of walkabouts during which each chief or officer would walk me around his spaces. In order to do these inspections properly, I'd ask them to bring me a flashlight.

It wasn't supposed to be a test, but the flashlights were pitiful. Broken, dead batteries, dim bulbs—you couldn't see anything. I figured this was what Commodore Kenny was talking about. I got myself a super Maglite that took four D-cell batteries. Its light was as bright as the sun. I carried that flashlight around with me everywhere. Soon, others started carrying flashlights that actually worked as well.

I attended a department head meeting, a routine review of maintenance issues, in the wardroom. The wardroom is a small room in which there's a ten-man table where the officers eat. It also serves as a training room, an operational planning room, a meeting room, and the place where officers watch movies. If necessary, it serves as the surgical operating room as well.

I looked around at the four department heads. These were the key individuals I would go to war with, entrust the lives of the 135 crew members to, and possibly die with. I felt bad for these guys: the attendees wandered in late, and the captain stayed away until everyone was assembled. Then he was invited. The meeting started late. It might seem like a little thing, but on board a nuclear submarine, little things like lack of punctuality are indicative of much, much bigger problems. At this particular meeting, everyone was waiting for someone else.

The meeting started. Lieutenant Dave Adams, the weapons officer (Weps), briefed a problem with the vertical launch system (VLS) in the bow of the sub. There was a long discussion about O-rings, seals, and retests. I probably should have paid attention to the technical issues because this missile system wasn't on the *Olympia* so I hadn't paid attention to it during my training, but instead I observed the people in the room. Dave was earnest and forthright but frustrated and defensive about all the questions he needed to answer. The other department heads and chiefs were bored.

After the meeting I followed Dave to his stateroom.

"Weps, you seemed a bit frustrated."

"Look, Captain, I have a vision of how I want this department to operate," he began. As I listened to him tell me about how he wanted things to be, I became more and more enthusiastic, and impressed. Unfortunately, he was being ignored. As he ticked through the ideas he had for improving his department, I would ask how he had implemented them. Each time the answer was the same: someone up the chain of command hadn't supported the initiative, so nothing happened. The chiefs working for him didn't seem eager to step up with their own ideas either. He had wanted to conduct training with the officers numerous times on Tomahawk missile strikes, something we would be tested on in January, but the training either had never been scheduled or had been canceled.

In essence, Dave was describing a problem inherent in the leader-follower model, although he didn't use those words. Because of his insights and passion he would become one of *Santa Fe*'s greatest engines for good, embracing the concept of leader-leader and carrying it forward.

I found Dave an incredibly intelligent, driven, and gifted officer. He grew up the younger son of a career Army enlisted man. Likely influenced by his demanding father, Dave acquired a drive I've rarely seen equaled. He also learned to appreciate his men but at the same time demand excellence from them. I felt better about my plan because I was going to have to rely on the technical expertise of Dave and the other department heads if it was going to work.

Dave wasn't the only frustrated officer. Lieutenant Commander Bill Greene, the navigator (Nav) and senior department head, had requested a transfer out of the submarine force. Two of the junior officers had submitted their resignations.

As things on *Santa Fe* deteriorated, the crew adopted a hunker-down mode in which avoiding mistakes became the primary driver for all actions. They focused exclusively on satisfying the minimum requirements. Anything beyond that was ignored.

During one of my walks around, I noted that one junior sailor looked particularly forlorn. When I pressed him on how he was doing, he told me he wasn't sure he was going to get home to the mainland for Christmas because his leave chit wasn't back yet. Turns out he'd submitted it weeks earlier and the holiday break was coming soon. He hadn't bought airline tickets yet since he didn't know if his leave would be approved, and now, this late, the tickets were bound to be expensive, if they were even available.

The Standard Submarine Organization and Regulations Manual (SSORM) states that the XO will sign all enlisted leave chits (and the CO all officer leave chits). Since we enforce the chain of command, that means that a leave chit from a junior sailor must go though his leading first class petty officer, divisional chief, department chief, chief of the boat, division officer, department head, and, finally, the XO. Seven people! The form had only five lines for signatures, so we were using rulers to half-split some of the lines so everyone could sign.

We had done this sailor wrong.

I rushed about, tracked down his leave chit—it was sitting in someone's inbox—and took care of it. It was the system, not the people, that failed, however.

Once I had acquainted myself with my men, I devoted time to observing some of the ship's routines. One morning I was talking to the engineer (Eng), Lieutenant Commander Rick Panlilio, when the radioman arrived with the message board. In those days, we took all the naval messages that came to the ship each day—there might be thirty or forty—printed them out, and routed them on a clipboard with a routing stamp. The stamp had a spot for each person to initial indicating he had seen the messages. Some messages were general and administrative, announcing courses or changes in requirements for paperwork or updates to manuals. Some messages were material, reporting changes in maintenance procedures or requesting data on a particular valve if made by a particular company. Some messages were operational, providing direction for the ship's schedule, assigning navigational waterspace, and tasking the ship for operations.

Rick flipped through the sheets of paper and was visibly

aggravated. "Here, look at this," he said. By protocol the messages are routed first to the captain, then to the XO, and down the chain of command. This way, the captain would be the first to know of any change in the ship's schedule. It is how we controlled the information.

The message board had already been to the captain and XO. Many of the messages had notes on them from one or both: things like "Enter this message change in the publication," or "I want a report back on this by Friday." Rick looked downcast. "See, this message is an urgent change to a publication; you don't think we know that we are supposed to enter the change? I'm getting told to do stuff before I even know I have stuff to do!"

"Why do you think the captain and XO feel they need to write those things?"

"Well, look, I may be wrong, but let's say something doesn't happen—some report does not get sent or a school date changes and we don't catch it—and some inspection team is looking at the records. The captain can say, 'I told him to do it,' and bully for him. He gets good marks for being very involved, having his fingerprints everywhere. But from my perspective, it's not helpful; it actually hurts. Not only are they telling me to do stuff I already know I have to do, but also frequently I get told exactly how and when to do it. That takes away any decision-making opportunities I might have."

As was the case with the message board, like every other submarine, *Santa Fe* had quarters on the pier a couple times a week. This was a morning formation with the crew standing behind their chiefs and officers in a square. The CO, XO, and chief of the boat (the senior enlisted man, known as the COB) were in the middle and made announcements. On the day I'm describing, we conducted an awards ceremony. It was great to see some sailors getting well-deserved recognition. The awards were for people leaving the ship or for the previous upkeep. Unfortunately, no wives had been invited to attend, and there was no photographer, so we lost the chance to promote these accomplishments in front of a wider audience. There was a last-minute scramble to assemble the citations and medals. We welcomed new crew members and bid aloha to departing ones. The captain seemed unfamiliar with the details about the men: where they had come from, where they were going.

As the formation went on, I wandered around the periphery. Standing in the back, where most of the crew was, I couldn't make out anything the captain said. His words were muted and garbled. I asked one of the crew members if he could hear. No, but it didn't matter, he said. If there was something important, the chief would tell them at divisional quarters, a meeting that followed this meeting. With leader-follower it didn't matter.

The overwhelming sense on the ship was that we needed to avoid problems: avoid drunken driving citations, avoid liberty incidents, avoid physical fitness failures, avoid tagout errors, avoid rework, and avoid a reactor problem.

Still, there was a spark, a desire to do well despite all these frustrations.

It was clear to me that whereas the *Olympia* crew wasn't as good as they thought they were, the *Santa Fe* crew wasn't as bad as they thought they were. There was a thirst to do better and an eagerness for change.

I felt the crew's pain and frustration in a physical way. When I arrived in the morning, my stomach was in knots as I anticipated finding out about some new way the crew's time was being wasted and their talents ignored. At the same time, I knew that their pain and frustration were providing me with a tremendous call to action. There would be an eagerness to change the way we were doing business that I could tap into. I resolved that we would turn everything on its head. I'd try the initiatives I had tried unsuccessfully on *Will Rogers*.

I went back to Commodore Kenny and told him I could definitely work with this. We would deploy on time.

QUESTIONS TO CONSIDER

- Is there a call to action in your organization?
- Do people want to change, or are they comfortable with the current level of performance?
- Are things too comfortable?
- Is there a feeling of complacency?
- Do people take action to protect themselves or to make the outcome better? Does leadership in your organization take control or give control?

"Whatever They Tell Me to Do!"

What goes on in your workplace every day that reinforces the notion that the guys at the top are the leaders and everyone else is simply to follow? I was startled to find this was pervasive on *Santa Fe*.

December 26, 1998: On Board USS *Santa Fe*, Pearl Harbor, Hawaii (fourteen days to change of command)

It was a quiet day over Christmas break. Only a skeleton watch section remained on board, and they were not doing any maintenance. The men were just taking logs and completing daily routines like loading potable water and pumping the sanitary tanks.

I wandered about the ship with my flashlight and made my way to the engine room. En route I passed the maneuvering room, which is the control room for the reactor and the propulsion plant. Formality here is to be stressed at all times. All personnel must ask permission to enter. It doesn't matter how senior you are; even admirals have to ask to be admitted. To be informal in the maneuvering room is detrimental to the safe operation of the ship, and thus a huge taboo.

I recalled the photo I had seen during PCO training that showed a bunch of shaggy-looking guys. They weren't just informal; they were cracking up. To make matters worse, this picture had gone around the Internet, and you could see in the background some of the dials and instruments for the reactor plant. The point of showing us the photograph during PCO training was to demonstrate how bad things could get without proper enforcement of standards. And, yes, the guys in the photo were crewmen on board *Santa Fe*.

I recognized some of the watch standers from the picture. I wondered if they knew how famous, or infamous, they were. Probably not. I stopped to chat with a first class petty officer on watch in the engine room. First class petty officers are one rank below chief. They are the workhorses of the Navy, doing a tremendous amount of watch standing, hands-on maintenance, as well as training of the junior enlisted men. They are considered to be budding leaders.

"Hi, what do you do on board?" By asking open-ended questions like this, I could better gauge what the crew thought their job was.

"Whatever they tell me to do," he immediately replied with unmistakable cynicism. He knew he was a follower, and not happy with it, but he also was not taking responsibility. He was throwing it back in my face that the command was all screwed up. It was a stunningly insulting thing to say, yet a brilliantly clear description of the problem. I should have been irate. Instead I felt strangely detached—like a scientific observer.

"Whatever they tell me to do." That was the attitude all over the ship. I began to see things in a new light.

Whatever They Tell Me to Do!

Toward the end of one day, I was sitting with the XO in his state-room. Lieutenant Commander Bill Greene, the navigator, came in and asked the XO if he had anything more for him that day. The XO, who was caught off guard by this question, said no and Bill headed home. Bill was, like everyone else on board, ready to do whatever he was told.

This was a show for me. I asked the XO if checking out was normal practice. In a proud voice, he told me that he liked the department heads to check out with him so he could go over what they "owed" and make sure they didn't go home with a significant issue open. But, he admitted, they didn't always do it.

I subsequently went over this end-of-day checkout event in detail with all the officers. The problem, I explained, was that in this scenario the XO is the one who was being responsible for each department head's work, not the department head himself. Psychological ownership for accomplishing the work rested with the XO, not the department head. Checking out is fine, I said, but it should go more like this: "XO, I'm shoving off for the day. The charts for next week's underway are coming along fine, and we'll be able to show the rough plan to the captain tomorrow. I wasn't able to see Petty Officer Smith for his qualification interview but will be able to make that up tomorrow." In this scenario, it is the department head, not the XO, who is responsible for the department head's job. This is leadership at all levels.

The department heads identified a potential problem with this approach. Who would be responsible and accountable for the work? If you, the captain, allow us to make decisions about the work, aren't you risking your professional reputation and career on how well we do? Isn't that the reason these ideas are so hard to implement?

They had a point. I pondered that. Would I be willing to be vulnerable to the effects of their decisions? On a submarine, a warship, there were lives at stake after all, not just our careers. I would retain accountability for *Santa Fe*'s operational performance but release control of the actual decisions to the department heads. It felt uncomfortable, but we were in such a bind that I didn't see any other way. Besides, *Santa Fe* was already at the bottom—how much worse could the ship do?

By contrast, "whatever they tell me to do" pointed to the reality that the fundamental structure of leader-follower was the problem on board ship. Everyone below the captain and the department heads had their brain shut off. What did that give us? We had 135 men on board and only 5 of them fully engaged their capacity to observe, analyze, and problem-solve. An image from my hometown popped into my head. I grew up in Concord, Massachusetts, near Lowell, where a host of empty textile mills mark the landscape. This is how I pictured the mental utilization of the crew—sitting idle.

Another thing bothered me as well. Who, exactly, was the "they" in the statement "whatever they tell me to do"? Wasn't "they" us?

Once I understood the pervasive influence that our structure of leader-follower had on our way of doing business, I saw examples of it everywhere I looked: in the way we conducted operations, the end-of-day checkout, the structure of the meetings, the routing of the message boards, the quarters on the pier.

Everything we did reinforced the notion that the guys at the top were the leaders and the rest of the crew were the followers. The problem for *Santa Fe* wasn't an absence of leadership. It was too much leadership of the wrong kind, the leader-follower kind.

I could also see the costs of leader-follower in the passivity of the sailors at quarters, in the lack of initiative, in the waiting for others, in the department heads' paralysis without the CO at the department head meetings.

Everything would have to change.

QUESTIONS TO CONSIDER

- Why is doing what you are told appealing to some?
- Do people really just want to do as they are told?
- If a snapshot of your business went viral on the Internet, what would it reveal about your workers?
- Do your procedures reinforce the leader-follower model?
- How would your middle managers react if you implemented a checkout system like the one described in this chapter?

"I Relieve You!"

s your organization spending more energy trying to avoid errors than achieving excellence? We were.

January 8, 1999: Submarine Base, Pearl Harbor
(172 days to deployment)

Freshly painted, *Santa Fe* sat proudly next to the pier at Submarine Base Pearl Harbor. The January weather was beautiful: sunny, 75 degrees, and light trade winds. On board the ship a portable platform had been loaded with a podium and four chairs. I was sitting in the second chair, looking across to the pier where the crew, families, and submarine community of Pearl Harbor were sitting under tents. In a few minutes, I would be taking command of a nuclear-powered warship and instantly become responsible for the taxpayers' $2 billion investment and 135 men. I would be responsible for preparing the warship to take the fight to the enemy and return home. It was a daunting task. It had come faster than I could have imagined, and I certainly didn't feel ready.

The authorities and responsibilities of the commanding officer, or captain, are specified in U.S. Navy Regulations:

> The responsibility of the commanding officer for his or her command is absolute . . . While the commanding officer may, at his or her discretion, and when not contrary to law or regulations, delegate authority to subordinates for the execution of details, such delegation of authority shall in no way relieve the commanding officer of continued responsibility for the safety, well-being and efficiency of the entire command (Section 0802).[6]

Delegation is the exception, not the rule. This issue of absolute responsibility has been a fundamental aspect of naval service since the United States Navy was crafted in the image of the Royal Navy. If the ship started to sink right at that moment, I would not be responsible. If it started to sink an hour later, it would be my responsibility, 100 percent. I would be accountable. While that singular point of accountability is attractive in many ways, there is a downside. The previous commanding officer would not be held accountable. Thus, as I pointed out earlier, each CO is encouraged to maximize performance for his tour and his tour alone. There is no incentive or reward for developing mechanisms that enable excellence beyond your immediate tour. Imagine the impact of this on the thousands of decisions made by the commanding officers throughout the Navy.

For example, in Section 0851 in the Navy Regulations on action with the enemy, the CO is directed to take the following action:

> Before going into battle or action communicate to the officers of the command, if possible, his or her plans for battle or action and such other information as may be of operational value should any of them succeed to command.

It might seem amazing that we feel it necessary to tell commanding officers to communicate the battle plan to their subordinates before going into combat, "if possible." If the crew doesn't know and understand the battle plan before then, defeat is almost certain.

But those Navy regs are describing the top-down, aloof, leader-follower structure that naval officers learn. Leader-follower is the image that comes to mind when we think of the confident, resolute commanding officer boldly leading his crew into battle. We think this is good leadership.

As I sat there on the dais musing about what I was soon to be accountable for, I thought back to my introduction to *Santa Fe* and took stock of what we had going for us.

First, the crew wanted change, even if they didn't know quite how to do it. When I asked the men what I shouldn't change, what worked particularly well, I didn't get a lot of answers. The frustration, wasted hours, and mediocre results of the previous year had convinced them they needed to do something else. Ultimately, we were to introduce a way of doing business that would be different from what they'd experienced before and would spare them the pain they'd suffered earlier on board. Without the thirst for change it would have been difficult to get the crew to accept an entirely new way of thinking about leadership. This call to action would be necessary for the changes I had in mind.

Second, we had an incredibly supportive chain of command. My bosses, Commodore Mark Kenny and Rear Admiral Al Konetzni, Commander, Submarine Forces, Pacific (COMSUBPAC or CSP), were ready to give me all the encouragement I needed—and all the rope I needed to hang myself. They were outcome focused. They didn't care or need to know the specifics of what we were going to do as long as the evidence showed that the submarine was improving in performance, war-fighting capability, and morale. This was good because I'm not sure I could have articulated the path ahead, and even if I had, I'm not sure they would have bought it.

Third, my reliance on the crew for the specifics of how the boat operated prevented me from falling into old habits and the trap of leader-follower. I couldn't have operated that way if I'd wanted to. There were many times I had the impulse to give specific direction but I couldn't. Although I cursed my lack of technical knowledge, it prevented me from falling back on bad habits. In the past when I would interview a crew member about how something worked, I only acted curious because, in reality, I knew how it worked. Now, when I talked to the men on the ship, I actually was curious.

Finally, it seemed clear that the crew was in a self-reinforcing downward spiral where poor practices resulted in mistakes, mistakes resulted in poor morale, and poor morale resulted in avoiding initiative and going into a survival mode of doing only what was absolutely necessary. In order to break this cycle, I'd need to radically change the daily motivation by shifting the focus from avoiding errors to achieving excellence.

Mechanism: Achieve Excellence, Don't Just Avoid Errors

In the nuclear-powered submarine Navy we focus on errors. We track them, we report them, and we attempt to understand the reasons for them. There is a powerful and effective culture of open and honest discussion about what went wrong and what could have gone better. What happens then is that we evaluate ships based on the mistakes they make. Avoiding mistakes becomes the prime focus of the crew and leadership.

What happened with *Santa Fe*, however, was that the crew was becoming gun-shy about making mistakes. The best way not to make a mistake is not to do anything or make any decisions. It dawned on me the day I assumed command that focusing on avoiding errors is helpful for understanding the mechanics of procedures and detecting impending major problems before they occur, but it is a debilitating approach when adopted as the objective of an organization.

You are destined to fail. No matter how good you get at avoiding mistakes, you will always have errors on something as complex as a submarine. You might reduce the number and severity, but there will never be zero. They may be such minor errors as reading a gauge wrong or scheduling two conflicting events, but people always make mistakes. Thus, they always feel bad about themselves. In the same vein, success is a negative, an absence of failure, avoidance of a critique or an incident. Sadly, a common joke on *Santa Fe* was "Your reward is no punishment."

Focusing on avoiding mistakes takes our focus away from becoming truly exceptional. Once a ship has achieved success merely in the form of preventing major errors and is operating in a competent way, mission accomplished, there is no need to strive further.

I resolved to change this. Our goal would be excellence instead of error reduction. We would focus on exceptional operational effectiveness for the submarine. We would achieve great things.

Part of achieving excellence would be acquiring an intimate understanding of errors, that is, what caused them and what we needed to do to eliminate them. But that intimate understanding would not be the thing the crew needed to be thinking about as they reported for duty. Reducing mistakes would be an important side benefit to attaining our primary goal, achieving excellence. Excellence was going to be more than a philosophy statement pasted to the bulkhead; it was going to be how we lived, ate, and slept.

My thoughts turned sharply back to the present. I heard the outgoing CO come to the end of his speech. I stood, and with the words "I relieve you," became the commanding officer of *Santa Fe*.

I turned to Commodore Kenny and reported I had relieved as CO *Santa Fe*.

I was now totally accountable for *Santa Fe* and committed myself to that role with the following words:

> I believe the personal freedoms, respect for human dignity, and economic prosperity we enjoy in the United States are unique throughout the history of mankind and across the span of the globe.
>
> I believe that this is not a natural state but one which must be worked for relentlessly, and, if necessary, defended.
>
> I believe the men who sallied forth from these very piers in boats like *Tang*, *Wahoo*, and *Barb* were engaged in an honorable and worthwhile endeavor.
>
> I believe those eternally on patrol beyond the reef did not die in vain. The future depends upon those willing to continue that honorable and worthwhile endeavor. Accordingly, I reaffirm my vow to defend the Constitution of the United States against all enemies, foreign and domestic.
>
> Shipmates of *Santa Fe*, I will be proud to sail with you.
>
> Thank you.

I sat down.

I was ready to go to work. We were scheduled to deploy in 172 days. As I looked across at the officers, chiefs, and sailors assembled on the pier, I knew we should start in the middle. We would start with the chiefs.

Going to sea in a submarine, leaving your family for six months, is hard work. Honorable work, but hard work. These guys weren't going to become rich looting enemy ships; they weren't in it for themselves. Fear was pervasive and we needed to turn that around.

Connecting our day-to-day activities to something larger was a strong motivator for the crew. The connection was there but it had been lost. Instead, in ways large and small, I encountered situations where the crew's actions were motivated by following a checklist, pleasing an inspector, looking good, or some other variant of "avoiding problems."

I, we, needed everyone to see the ultimate purpose for the submarine and remember that it was a noble purpose. I also wanted to connect our current endeavors with the submarine force's rich legacy of service to and sacrifice for the country. Once the crewmen remembered what we were doing and why, they would do anything to support the mission. This was a stark contrast to earlier, when people were coming to work simply with the hope of not screwing up.

ACHIEVE EXCELLENCE, DON'T JUST AVOID ERRORS is a mechanism for CLARITY. (The book to read is Simon Sinek's *Start with Why*.)

QUESTIONS TO CONSIDER

- Are your people trying to achieve excellence or just to avoid making mistakes?
- Has your organization become action-averse because taking action sometimes results in errors?
- Have you let error-reduction programs sap the lifeblood out of initiative and risk taking?
- Do you spend more time critiquing errors than celebrating success?
- Are you able to identify the symptoms of avoiding errors in your workplace?
- When you ask people what their jobs are, do they answer in terms of reducing errors?

- When you investigate the criteria that went behind decisions, do you find that avoidance of negative outcomes far outweighs accomplishing positive outcomes?
- What is the primary motivation of the middle managers and rank and file (not what it says on the wall poster outside the boardroom)?
- How can you minimize errors but not make that the focus of your organization?

PART II

CONTROL

My primary focus when I assumed command of *Santa Fe* was to divest control and distribute it to the officers and crew. Control is about making decisions concerning not only how we are going to work but also toward what end.

A submarine has a built-in structure whereby information is channeled up the chain of command to decision makers. Instead, we were going to deconstruct decision authority and push it down to where the information lived. We called this "Don't move information to authority, move authority to the information."

The chapters in this part will introduce you to the initial set of mechanisms we devised to implement leader-leader practices. I've organized the mechanisms into three groups: control, competence, and clarity. Although the initial focus was on redistributing control, it was necessary to work in all three areas.

- Find the genetic code for control and rewrite it.
- Act your way to new thinking.

- Short, early conversations make efficient work.
- Use "I intend to . . ." to turn passive followers into active leaders.
- Resist the urge to provide solutions.
- Eliminate top-down monitoring systems.
- Think out loud (both superiors and subordinates).
- Embrace the inspectors.

Change, in a Word

What's the best way to change decision-making authorities in your organization? Turns out it's pretty easy once you commit to changing.

January 8, 1999: Old Periscope Facility,
Submarine Base, Pearl Harbor
(172 days to deployment)

Later that afternoon, I sat with the chiefs of *Santa Fe* in the defunct World War II periscope repair facility. Now a tired and unassuming two-story building next to the piers, this structure had once been a constant scene of activity as technicians worked to refurbish and focus the periscopes of American submarines. These were the tools that such men as Dick O'Kane, Mush Morton, and Gene Fluckey would use to achieve victory against the Empire of Japan. The periscope repair functions had moved to a larger and more up-to-date facility a hundred yards away, and the original facility was now an informal lounge. The room was hot and uncomfortable. We sat on recycled furniture with a squeaky ceiling fan turning slowly above us and the windows opened to let in the slight breeze.

If I started at the top, with the XO, COB, and department heads, we would be using a top-down approach to implement a bottom-up leadership philosophy. That was inherently contradictory. Additionally, that would involve only six people and wouldn't create a critical mass of participation. The junior officers weren't a good place to start because they had lost credibility in the command and would still have to learn the basics of leadership. Starting at the bottom, with the junior enlisted men, probably wouldn't work either. There was too much distance between them and me, and without support in the rest of the command, they would be viewed suspiciously. So here I was with the chiefs.

I had suffered through many wasted hours listening to lectures about how we should "work together," "take initiative," and the like. These weren't backed up with mechanisms that actually enabled or rewarded these behaviors, so the speeches were worse than nothing at all; they sounded hypocritical and the speakers out of touch.

I was resolved to avoid this altogether. Instead of trying to change mind-sets and then change the way we acted, we would start acting differently and the new thinking would follow. Or so I hoped. Besides, we didn't have time for a long gestation period. We needed change now!

I wasn't 100 percent sure that the chiefs would bite. I was confident in the support of the chief of the boat (COB). As the senior enlisted man, he was organizationally committed to supporting me. I was less confident about the rest. I was sorry that Senior Chief Andy Worshek, the senior sonarman and weapons department chief, was on leave. I knew he would have been an ally. I looked around; Chief John Larson, an electronics technician (ET), sat opposite me. He had struck me as thoughtful and eager to learn. Chief Brad Jensen, the senior nuclear chief (we called him the bull nuke), and his nuke chiefs sat together. They'd likely be on board.

I was glad to see Chief David Steele in the group. After our earlier conversation, he had gone home and talked to his wife. They agreed to give the new command a chance, and he withdrew his transfer request. His positive nodding was already influencing the men around him in a good way as the meeting began.

My flashlight was superfluous but I had brought it anyway. Brandishing it, I opened with a question: "Men, we say the chiefs run the Navy. Is this true on *Santa Fe*?"

Reflexively they answered, Yes! Uh-huh. Of course!

"Really?"

"Well . . ." came the second round of answers, as most of them looked at the floor. Apparently not so much on *Santa Fe*.

They were right. The chiefs did not run the Navy and they did not run the *Santa Fe*. The authority of the chief petty officers had long been eroded away. The reasons for this were both institutional and human. The institutional problem was that the desire to have the commanding officer uniquely and completely accountable for the ship ran counter to allowing the chiefs the authority to manage things. Admiral Hyman Rickover and the nuclear-powered Navy implemented a highly successful program with an unparalleled safety record. From an organizational perspective, the accountability of the commanding officers was heavily stressed. Their selection and training were incredibly important. The department heads approved operations, and the department head or captain authorized maintenance. A long list of activities and evolutions could be performed only with the specific permission of the CO, and so on.

These practices reinforced leader-follower in the submarine force. As a result, the performance of the submarines was directly coupled with the technical ability of the CO. As I've already mentioned, some ships would do well under one CO and then poorly under the next.

At the same time, the naval nuclear propulsion program has succeeded in developing an alternative to the personality-centered leadership approach: a procedurally centered leadership structure in which the procedure reigns supreme. This structure is effective when it comes to operating a nuclear reactor. The system is well defined and predictable: people are highly trained and the operators follow the procedure! Actually, as a citizen of the planet, you want this procedurally centered leadership when it comes to operating the reactor plant. The range of potential conditions and responses is bounded. It is when operators don't follow procedures that very unpredictable, and typically bad, things happen.

Yet this emphasis on following the procedure can have a stultifying effect. We take bright operators, train them extensively, and then tell them that the most important thing is to follow the procedure.

When it comes to operating a submarine against the enemy, the application of this procedurally centered approach is limiting, both in how the submarine is employed and in how the intellect of the operators is employed. Fundamentally, tactical operations of the submarine are different from reactor plant operations. Tactical operations are against an intelligent enemy who thinks, plots, and deliberately exploits weaknesses. The complexity is significantly higher. Strictly following procedures won't get us there. At this point, we fall back on the personality-centered leadership structure.

In reversing years of the leader-follower system's erosion of the chiefs' authority, the chiefs on board *Santa Fe*—now under my command—would be going against the grain. I wanted to make sure they deliberately decided to take charge. It wouldn't be any good if I directed them. You can't invoke leader-follower rules to direct a shift from leader-follower to leader-leader.

To say these guys were skeptical would be an understatement. Sure, they sensed that things could have been better but, after all, *Santa Fe* hadn't had a collision, grounding, or truly significant incident. Was it performing that poorly?

Furthermore, they'd been in the Navy for fifteen years, on average, and it had always been this way on all their other submarines. Was it possible that a better way existed?

My next question built on what we had all agreed on, namely, the chiefs did not run *Santa Fe*.

I asked, "Do you want to?"

Reflexively they answered, Yes! Uh-huh. Of course!

"Really?"

And that's when we began to talk honestly about what the chiefs' running the submarine would mean.

Mechanism: Find the Genetic Code for Control and Rewrite It

Here is a list of the primary problems the chiefs struggled with:

- Below-average advancement rates for their men
- A lengthy qualification program that yielded few qualified watch standers
- Poor performance on evaluations for the ship
- A lean watch bill, with many watch stations port and starboard under way, and three-section in port (the objective was to have three-section at sea and at least four-section in port; this meant that each member would stand watch every third watch rotation—typically six hours on watch and twelve hours off—at sea, and every fourth day in port)
- An inability to schedule, control, and commence work on time
- An inability to control the schedules of their division and men.

We talked about the reality that running *Santa Fe* would mean they would be accountable for the performance of their divisions. No more sitting in the cozy chiefs' quarters and letting the department head or division officer explain to the captain why things had gone wrong. Later, I would call this "eyeball accountability." It would mean being intimately involved—physically present in most cases—in the operations of the ship and in each activity.

The chiefs' enthusiasm waned noticeably. Some could see this would change the way they would have to think about their position: being the chief would no longer mean a position of privilege but a position of accountability, responsibility, and work. Not everyone thought this would be better. We discussed this long and hard, but didn't waste time discussing the philosophy of the role of the chief petty officer in today's Navy or on exhortations and speeches. We didn't have time for those luxuries.

At the end, we were agreed: the sole output would be concrete mechanisms. I was thinking about Jim Collins and Jerry Porras's book *Built to Last* and their discussion of how personalities come and go but institutional mechanisms endure and embed the change in the organization. I put this question to *Santa Fe*'s chiefs: "What can we do so that you actually run the ship?"

First and foremost, the chiefs wanted to be in charge of their own men, and that meant putting them in charge of their men's leave. Some of the chiefs protested, claiming they were already in charge of their leave. But after the COB signed the leave chit—and he did so for every enlisted man—it still needed to be signed by three officers: the division officer, the department head, and the XO. The chiefs weren't in charge.

The chiefs came up with a solution: could the COB be the final signature authority for the enlisted leave chits? It was brilliantly simple. Instead of making a fourteen-step process more efficient (seven steps up through the enlisted chain of command and the COB, to the division officer, department head, and XO, and seven steps down), we would eliminate six of the steps. I just needed to cross out XO and write in COB in the ship's regulations. A one-word change. That was the genetic code. That was what they were proposing.

I was reluctant to agree for a couple of reasons. In my previous jobs, I had countermanded ill-thought-out leave plans from the chiefs. Knowing the officers above them would likely veto excessive leave plans and wanting to be the nice guys, the chiefs tended to say "yes" a lot. Additionally, I was concerned that the junior officers would lose the experience of learning personnel management and lose touch with their divisions. Finally, and perhaps most important, the CO wasn't authorized to make this change. The submarine organization manual was a Navy document that we weren't supposed to change.

We discussed some of these drawbacks, and the chiefs offered their solution. The chiefs would be responsible for the performance of their divisions and all that encompassed. I agreed and made the change to the manual that afternoon. In command less than a day and I'd already exceeded my authority.

This one-word administrative change put the chiefs squarely in charge of all aspects of managing their men, including their watch bills, qualification schedules, and training school enrollments. The only way the chiefs could own the leave planning was if they owned the watch bill. The only way they could own the watch bill was if they owned the qualification process. It turned out that managing leave was only the tip of the iceberg and that it rested on a large supporting base of other work. It was hugely powerful. We called it "Chiefs in Charge."

Because we had just removed a significant amount of the XO's authority by eliminating him from the process of signing the enlisted leave chits, I needed to do something to show that I was walking the walk. Therefore, I delegated the control of all officer leave, which I was required to sign, to the XO. This was consistent with what we'd done with the chiefs, and also beyond my authority.

I wasn't worried about the authority issue, but I was worried about the behavior. If the chiefs continued to be the "good guys" and approve every chit that came their way, the interests of the command would not be protected. As it turned out, however, that didn't happen.

Find Your Organization's Genetic Code for Control

Here's an exercise you can do with your senior leadership at your next off-site.

- Identify in the organization's policy documents where decision-making authority is specified. (You can do this ahead of time if you want.)
- Identify decisions that are candidates for being pushed to the next lower level in the organization.
- For the easiest decisions, first draft language that changes the person who will have decision-making authority. In some cases, large decisions may need to be disaggregated.
- Next, ask each participant in the group to complete the following sentence on the five-by-eight card provided: "When I think about delegating this decision, I worry that . . ."
- Post those cards on the wall, go on a long break, and let the group mill around the comments posted on the wall.
- Last, when the group reconvenes, sort and rank the worries and begin to attack them.

When I've conducted this exercise, I usually find that the worries fall into two broad categories: issues of competence and issues of clarity. People are worried that the next level down won't make good decisions, either because they lack the technical competence about the subject or because they don't understand what the organization is trying to accomplish. Both of these can be resolved.

FIND THE GENETIC CODE AND REWRITE IT is a mechanism for CONTROL. The first step in changing the genetic code of any organization or system is delegating control, or decision-making authority, as much as is comfortable, and then adding a pinch more. This isn't an empowerment "program." It's changing the way the organization controls decisions in an enduring, personal way.

In the example I just shared, there was nothing technically complicated about signing a leave chit. The barriers had to do with trusting that the chiefs understood the goals of *Santa Fe* the way I did. I call this organizational clarity, or just clarity. (I describe this in greater detail in the chapters in Part IV.) You tackle it by being honest about what you intend to achieve and communicating that all the time, at every level.

Many empowerment programs fail because they are just that, "programs" or "initiatives" rather than the central principle—the genetic code, if you will—behind how the organization does business. You can't "direct" empowerment programs. Directed empowerment programs are flawed because they are predicated on this assumption: I have the authority and ability to empower you (and you don't). Fundamentally, that's disempowering. This internal contradiction dooms these initiatives. We say "empowerment" but do it in a way that is disempowering. The practice outweighs the rhetoric.

In a broader sense, this mechanism highlights the point that we didn't give speeches or discuss a philosophical justification for the changes we were going to make. Rather, we searched for the organizational practices and procedures that would need to be changed in order to bring the change to life with the greatest impact. My goal, professionally and personally, was to implement enduring mechanisms that would embed the goodness of the organization in the submarine's people and practices and wouldn't rely on my personality to make it happen.

We expanded the power of the chiefs several times during the three years I was on *Santa Fe*. We started with giving them control over their men's leave. The next iteration was to make sure there was a chief who was in charge of every evolution. I wanted to make sure it was clear whenever something happened on the submarine that some chief was responsible for making sure it came out right. The mechanism was to add a line to our planning documents that listed the "Chief in Charge" next to each event. I learned that focusing on who was put in charge was more important than trying to evaluate all the ways the event could go wrong. These "Chiefs in Charge" initiatives were instrumental in *Santa Fe*'s winning the award for the best chiefs' quarters for the next seven years in a row.

We discovered that distributing control by itself wasn't enough. As that happened, it put requirements on the new decision makers to have a higher level of technical knowledge and clearer sense of organizational purpose than ever before. That's because decisions are made against a set of criteria that includes what's technically appropriate and what aligns with the organization's interests. In later chapters, you'll be introduced to mechanisms that address both of these supporting pillars.

QUESTIONS TO CONSIDER

- How can you prepare your mid-level managers to shift from holding a "position of privilege" to one of "accountability, responsibility, and work"?

- What procedure or process can you change with one word that will give your mid-level managers more decision-making authority?
- When thinking about delegating control, what do you worry about?
- What do you as a proponent of the leader-leader approach need to delegate to show you are willing to walk the talk?

"Welcome Aboard Santa Fe!"

Don't like something about the "culture" in your organization and want to change it? We did this in a simple way.

January 11, 1999: Pearl Harbor, Hawaii
(169 days to deployment)

The buzz of excitement filled the air on board the USS *Santa Fe* Monday morning as the chiefs started talking about their new authority. The sailors took notice and, accordingly, there was more spring in their step as we went about the work of the day. It seemed that the direct connection between the chiefs, who were responsible for making the work come out right, and the sailors, who were the performers of the valve lineups, maintenance procedures, and operational tasks, had engaged both the troops and the supervisors alike. There was greater commitment, greater engagement.

Military discipline improved as well. In the past, some of the junior enlisted men would mouth off to their chiefs. (We called this showing "attitude," which is not a good thing.) Since each chief's authority to discipline them for their remarks was minimal, these puerile enlisted men could afford to complain; the cost was low. Now, with the chiefs' having more authority, the junior enlisted men were motivated to suppress their immature responses and get to the work of the day. So far, so good.

Overall, the mood was upbeat. Yet there was so much to do. We were deploying in 169 days; more urgently, prior to deployment there would be a series of inspections of increasing complexity. We were scheduled to get under way in eight days to do the first of these: an inspection conducted by my immediate superior, Commodore Mark Kenny. He and his squadron staff were going to be riding us for four days, observing *Santa Fe* perform a host of submarine operations.

I wasn't sure how we could possibly do well. The knowledge gaps were so big and the operational practice so rusty there was no way we could learn and practice everything we needed to do in the next week. Besides, we had a full 24/7 job just finalizing the repairs and maintenance from the past month, loading stores, and preparing the charts and operational plan to get under way on time.

Not only did we need to demonstrate to the squadron staff that we were competent; we needed a success in support of the changes I needed to make because not everyone understood how this new scheme was going to work. I already had skeptics among the crew.

I tried to understand the skeptics' position. One thing that bothered them was that this way of doing business was different from what they had been doing before—on *Santa Fe* and on every other submarine in the force. There were two components to this. First, many of the chiefs had served on two, three, or even four submarines. No one else had authorized the COB to be the final authority on enlisted leave. Heck, they'd never even heard of it. Was it possible that a way of doing business no one had ever heard of could be better than what the Navy had been doing for more than one hundred years? It was a legitimate question.

Second, there was the fear and cost of being different. Even if we demonstrated that this was a better way, did we want to operate differently from the other fifty-five nuclear-powered attack submarines in the Navy? Several advisers asked me point-blank if I was willing to take the career risk. "Why don't you just be like everyone else, do the normal things, build teamwork, enforce standards, conduct training?" they'd suggest. "If things go well with your new program, great, but if things don't go well, there will be a long line of people saying, 'Well, he did things differently from the rest of us.'"

Chalk it up to being left-handed, perhaps, but I didn't feel any of this fear myself. As I thought about it, pushing authority down could only be good. I remembered how I had felt on board the *Sunfish* when my CO let me run my own watch team and how powerful that was. I remembered how I had reverted to top-down leadership on the *Will Rogers* as well, and how dispiriting that was.

Right or wrong, I was committed to doing whatever I thought was best for *Santa Fe*, the Navy, and the nation without worrying about the repercussions. I called this the paradox of "caring but not caring"—that is, caring intimately about your subordinates and the organization but caring little about the organizational consequences to yourself.

Despite the skeptics, enough of the team was willing to try our new approach and give me the benefit of the doubt. Some were enthusiastically sold and formed the core of advocates. The skeptics were willing to give it a shot, although less enthusiastically. They weren't going to get in the way.

The morning wardroom meeting was my first substantive session with the officers. I had told them to bring all the leave chits they had in their inboxes, and I collected them at the meeting to give to the COB. The pile of unapproved leave chits was significant and provided a physical context for the changes we were making. We had an initiative going for the chiefs, but I wanted to come up with something for the entire ship. The officers would help me craft it.

Mechanism: Act Your Way to New Thinking

One of the things I heard during my turnover discussions was that they wanted to change the morale among the crew. We invest an average of $50,000 to recruit a sailor, then another $100,000 to train a submarine sailor and give that individual significant responsibility at sea. On board *Santa Fe*, almost none of the enlisted men had stayed beyond their initial tour of duty. Of a crew of 135, only 3 sailors reenlisted in 1998. Two of the junior officers, who are trained at an even greater cost, had already submitted their resignations.

How do you raise morale quickly? It didn't seem like you could just order a cultural change like this. And yet, that's just what we did.

I asked the officers how we would know if the crew were proud of the boat. What would we observe? There was silence. Apparently these officers weren't accustomed to being involved. I pointed my flashlight at one of the junior officers. "You go first," I commanded, and after he spoke, others volunteered their own opinions:

- They'd brag about it to their family and friends!
- They'd look visitors in the eye when they met them in the passageway!
- They'd wear their *Santa Fe* ball caps as much as possible!
- They'd boast to their friends on other submarines!
- They'd buy *Santa Fe* lighters, pens, and pins from the ship's store!

Well, what if we just tell them to act that way? I suggested. What if we just tell them to greet people respectfully, sincerely, and proudly? Could we act, or talk, our way into a new way of thinking?

This sparked a vigorous debate. Some thought that would be

like putting the cart before the horse. First, we needed to create a work environment that would give the men respect and dignity; a place they were happy to go to each day. Then behavior would change, and morale would improve naturally, on its own. Others thought we could talk ourselves into it, almost fake it.

I decided we would try the route of talking ourselves into a new way of thinking. We called it the "three-name rule" and this is how it worked: When any member of the crew saw a visitor on our boat (and we were specifically thinking about the following week, when Commodore Kenny and his staff were coming down for the inspection), he was to greet the visitor using three names—the visitor's name, his own name, and the ship's name. For example, "Good morning, Commodore Kenny, my name is Petty Officer Jones, welcome aboard *Santa Fe*."

On the pier at quarters the next day, I started explaining the three-name rule to the crew. Almost immediately I stopped; as was normal, the crew stood in formation behind the officers and chiefs and I knew that most of those in the back couldn't hear what I was saying. I waved my arms and shouted, "Gather round." It wasn't in the book of commands, but everyone knew what I wanted. The men moved forward. Now I was in a tight and intimate huddle of a hundred men. It wasn't something General Patton would have been proud of, but it definitely seemed better. The officers and chiefs were still in front, but because I interacted with that group frequently, I sent them to the back. From that moment on, at quarters the crew would gather around me and the khakis (officers and chiefs) would stand in back.

I went on to tell the crew what we wanted going forward. We had seven days to finish putting the boat back together and head to sea. We had torpedoes to prepare, maintenance to complete, repairs to finish, charts to prepare, stores to load, and a number of other things to accomplish. So, I resisted giving a big lecture about the reasons why we wanted to use the three-name rule and about respecting their time and their need to get back to work. Instead, I just explained the rule and acted it out.

How to Embed a Cultural Change in Your Organization

Starting condition: you've had a discussion with your leadership group and identified some sort of cultural change the group mostly agrees to. What you want to do now is embed it into the organization, independent of personality.

- Hand out five-by-eight cards. Have people complete the following sentence: "I'd know we achieved [this cultural change] if I saw employees . . ." (The specific wording in this question should move you from general, unmeasurable answers like "Have people be creative" to specific, measurable ones like "Employees submit at least one idea a quarter. The ideas are posted and other employees can comment on them.")
- Allow five minutes. Then tape the cards on the wall, go on break, and have everyone mill around reading the cards.
- Based on the discussions and quantity of answers, you may want to give everyone a second shot at filling out the cards.
- Sort and prioritize the answers.
- Then discuss how to code the behavior into the company's practices. For example: implementing the three-name rule.
- The final step is to write the new practices into the appropriate company procedure.

When you're trying to change employees' behaviors, you have basically two approaches to choose from: change your own thinking and hope this leads to new behavior, or change your behavior and hope this leads to new thinking. On board *Santa Fe*, the officers and I did the latter, acting our way to new thinking. We didn't have time to change thinking and let that percolate and ultimately change people's actions; we just needed to change the behavior. Frankly, I didn't care whether people thought differently at some point—and they eventually did—so long as they behaved in certain ways. I think there were likely some sailors who never understood what we were trying to do and resisted the change to leader-leader, but they behaved as if they believed.

Some observers attributed the low morale on *Santa Fe* to the long hours. I didn't think so. I felt it had more to do with focusing on reducing errors instead of accomplishing something great and the resultant feeling of ineffectiveness that had permeated the ship.

The sense on board was that we were not proactive movers but only passive reactors to external events. The schedule was against us, the parts didn't arrive on time, the detailers didn't give *Santa Fe* sailors the jobs they wanted, the torpedo missed because of "bad luck." There was an emphasis on blaming what was happening on outside influences and factors, and the crew evidenced a collective lack of responsibility. This feeling of victimhood went hand in hand with the low morale. One of the things the three-name rule accomplished was that it got rid of that sense of being victims of our circumstances. In a small way, each sailor on board *Santa Fe* was now taking charge of his destiny.

ACTING YOUR WAY TO NEW THINKING is a mechanism for CONTROL.

QUESTIONS TO CONSIDER

- How do you respond when people in your workplace don't want to change from the way things have always been done?
- What are some of the costs associated with doing things differently in your industry?
- Do we act first, and think later? Or do we think first, and then change our actions?

Under Way on Nuclear Power

Do you play "bring me a rock" in your organization, where vague understanding of the goal results in wasted time? We did, and we needed to change that.

January 20, 1999: Pearl Harbor, Hawaii (160 days to deployment)

I'd been in command twelve days. The sun was getting low on the horizon as I fidgeted on the bridge of *Santa Fe*. We were awaiting the clearance message from the maintenance facility that approved the repairs we'd made and authorized us to get under way. That the message was late was our fault. A couple of minor retests had held us up; nothing as bad as on board the *Will Rogers*, though. The tugboat was made up alongside. Much longer and we'd have had to delay a day before setting to sea. That would knock out one of our four days of preparation before we came in to pick up Commodore Mark Kenny and the inspection team.

The speaker on the bridge crackled. "Captain, XO, clearance message on board."

The officer of the deck (OOD) turned to me. "Captain, all departments report readiness to get under way. Request permission to get under way."

"Get under way!" I responded.

The tug pulled the bow away from the pier, and we silently slipped into the channel and headed to sea. The magic of the moment when the ship has cast off the last lines both to shore and to the tug never loses its potency. That particular moment was no exception.

This was great fun. When I gave orders, big things happened! I would say "submerge the ship" and we would dive under the ocean. "Ahead flank" and *Santa Fe* surged through the water, "Bring the ship to periscope depth" and officers executed a procedure to safely bring *Santa Fe* just under the surface of the Pacific Ocean.

This was welcome action in contrast to the previous weeks' trials. In addition to the material issues of putting the boat back together, we had some struggles in preparing ourselves operationally. The crew was still focusing too much on complying with regulations rather than working to make our submarine the most operationally capable warship possible. It was the same problem as focusing on avoiding mistakes instead of trying to achieve something great. A typical example involved the preparation of the underway charts.

Perfect, but Irrelevant

Nautical charts are the foundation for nuclear submarine operations. They serve as maps, showing the routes we must follow to avoid buoys, shallows, and other submarines while at the same time achieving our operational objectives. In the upcoming exercise, we had to locate an enemy submarine, monitor its activities, and if directed, sink it. We knew the focus of the operations would be in the Maui basin—the area between Maui, Lanai, and Molokai. It is an area of shallow water and has an uneven bottom that makes submarining there difficult.

Chart preparations consisted of three phases. In phase one, the quartermasters took the large paper charts and made sure they were up-to-date with information from the latest Coast Guard–issued "Notice to Mariners." There might be additional hazards to navigation, such as the setting or moving of a buoy, since the submarine last moved through those waters. In addition, the paper charts had to be prepared according to submarine force instructions, such as highlighting the one-hundred-fathom curve and marking points ten miles from shoal water and twelve miles from land.

Phase two consisted of laying out our assigned water. Since submarines are large, quiet objects, we assign them different blocks of water so they can move safely without fear of collisions. These blocks designate depth zones and geographic zones and change throughout the day and week. It's imperative that these charts be absolutely correct; otherwise, you might inadvertently operate in water assigned to another submarine, risking collision. If you discovered yourself in this position, you would surface immediately and report the incident.

The third, final phase consisted of integrating the operational plan with the chart. This involved laying down a track within the assigned water to accomplish the anticipated mission. This included the specific courses, speeds, and depth zones *Santa Fe* would use.

The charts then went through a laborious review process starting with the quartermasters who prepared them and moving up through the assistant navigator (ANAV), the navigator (Lieutenant Commander Bill Greene), and with final approval by the captain—me.

In response to a recent navigational problem on another submarine, a force-wide directive had added the XO, second in command, to the review process. The Navy commonly added such steps for the force to perform in order to prevent recurrence. (Steps are rarely removed.) Unfortunately, often these additional steps don't prevent recurrence and sometimes make matters worse. It's like adding inspectors at the end of the process to see if it's gone well—extra work without making anything better.

As the time for underway got closer, I became anxious because I hadn't seen the charts. Bill Greene kept telling me they were "almost ready." Finally, on Sunday, with underway scheduled for Tuesday, he called me to say he was ready to review the charts.

After all those steps in the review process, they were perfect—but irrelevant.

The charts were perfect in that they complied with all the rules and regulations. No inspector could have found a deficiency. They were irrelevant because even though the review team factored in where the operational plan had the submarine going, I knew we wouldn't be using the route they proposed.

The quartermasters who prepared the charts knew we would end up in the Maui basin, but they didn't know which of the three paths we'd take to get there: north of Molokai, between Molokai and Lanai, or south of Lanai. They plotted the navigationally better route, which was north of Molokai. This was open water and the fastest route, but it wasn't the way the enemy submarine would go and, hence, wasn't the way we needed to go.

None of the reviews up the chain of command noted this problem because the reviews were all focused on making sure the charts were navigationally and procedurally correct, not on enabling *Santa Fe* to be an operationally effective warship. In short, the reviews were focused on avoiding errors, as opposed to accomplishing something.

There was another human tendency working against us as well. Subordinates generally desire to present the boss with a "perfect" product the first time. Unfortunately, this gets in the way of efficiency because significant effort can be wasted. We decided then and there that at each phase in the review process the navigator or the assistant navigator should talk to me. These would be quick conversations. On their part, the review team needed to overcome a fear of criticism of an incomplete plan; on my part, I needed to refrain from jumping in with answers. We boiled this down to this motto: "A little rudder far from the rocks is a lot better than a lot of rudder close to the rocks."

Mechanism: Short, Early Conversations Make Efficient Work

Not everyone liked this idea. Getting me, the boss, involved in the process risked my losing my level of detachment and being less willing to scrap the plan and start over because I had been part of its development. At this point, that was a trade-off I was willing to take because I sensed I needed frequent conversations with all levels of the chain of command to ensure that they were working toward accomplishing operational excellence. Later, once the crew had adopted the new philosophy of achieving operational excellence rather than avoiding errors, I would back out of the process.

Beyond this hurdle was another, more basic, problem. The charts were inconsistently drawn. On one chart, the one-hundred-fathom curve was highlighted in yellow, on another, red.

The young officers responsible for executing the ship's mission standing watch as OOD would be presented with different chart legends on different charts and on different days. Yellow would mean something here, something different there. I also imagined running to look at the chart in the middle of the night in a dark control room and not being able to quickly sort out the picture because we hadn't consistently applied color to the charts. These situations spelled nothing but disaster.

Angry that the reviews hadn't focused on the right operational goals, I instinctively wanted to grab the XO and demand improvement. He'd in turn grab Bill Greene, who would grab Chief John Larson and the ANAV, and so on. We'd be adhering to the chain of command, but with only forty-eight hours to get under way, it wouldn't have gotten us ready in time. Further, it would perpetuate the top-down approach I was trying to get away from.

Instead, we gathered all the quartermasters to discuss the issues. I thought the junior sailors would be huffy about being called into a big meeting with the captain when all they wanted was to get the work done. I was wrong.

I laid out my issues with the charts and how I'd come to the conclusions I came to. One of the junior quartermasters, recently qualified to stand watch, was a stocky African-American we called Sled Dog because he would work till he dropped. If you just met him walking through the ship, you would have guessed he was an auxiliaryman, not a quartermaster.

To my surprise, Sled Dog immediately perked up and began offering suggestions. He had clearly been frustrated, toiling away in the dark; now he had a voice. It was a classic case of the workers' being technically competent but unclear about what we were trying to achieve. This inefficient work practice was the antithesis of what we were going to do, and I was glad to have this insight.

When asked about the significance of the different colors chosen for the contour lines, Sled Dog frankly admitted that the curves were highlighted simply based on what colored markers were available at the time.

I wanted the colors to be consistent and to convey information. Someone suggested that we use a modified *National Geographic* scheme: shades of red would represent shallow water, shades of blue deeper water. We also came up with standard schemes for water assignments. *Santa Fe*'s water would always be blue in military exercises (American forces are always "blue"); other submarines would be yellow; areas where we shared water but were separated by depth zone would be—you guessed it—green! A quick look at the chart and each OOD would know instantly that if it was blue, *Santa Fe* owned the water; if it was yellow, we needed to stay out; and if it was green, we needed to maintain a specific depth zone. This worked because the display conventions in efficient symbology and coloring tapped a much larger body of knowledge in your brain. It built on what you already knew. (The book to read on this subject is Edward Tufte's *The Visual Display of Quantitative Information*.)

We tried the changes, and after agreeing that they made sense Bill Greene wrote our new procedures up in the Standing Orders. This is where excellence in navigation occurred and where excellence in combat effectiveness started.

SHORT, EARLY CONVERSATIONS is a mechanism for CONTROL. It is a mechanism for control because the conversations did not consist of me telling them what to do. They were opportunities for the crew to get early feedback on how they were tackling problems. This allowed them to retain control of the solution. These early, quick discussions also provided clarity to the crew about what we wanted to accomplish. Many lasted only thirty seconds, but they saved hours of time.

A commanding officer's attention is no doubt highly valuable time for the organization, and the hierarchy was supposed to protect that time. Inefficiencies in my time were highly visible, especially to me. Less visible, however, were the inefficiencies of all the people throughout the organization. In my organization, even accounting for the difference in the value of our time, those inefficiencies overwhelmingly outweighed whatever efficiency I was getting with my time as captain.

Furthermore, supervisors needed to recognize that the demand for perfect products the first time they see them results in significant waste and frustration throughout their organization. Even a thirty-second check early on could save your people numerous hours of work. Many, many times I'd be walking around the boat and ask someone, "Show me what you are working on," only to discover that a well-meaning yet erroneous translation of intent was resulting in a significant waste of resources.

Don't You Trust Me?

One problem that came up as we spread the idea of these short interactions earlier in the process was the question of trust. I could hear the petty officers complaining that the command "didn't trust them," and sometimes they challenged me directly with that complaint. For a long time this bothered me because I actually did trust them, but I didn't know how to answer the question. Then I realized that we were talking about two totally different things.

Trust means this: when you report that we should position the ship in a certain position, *you believe* we should position the ship as you indicated. Not trusting you would mean that I thought you might be saying one thing while *actually* believing something else. Trust is purely a characteristic of the human relationship. Now, whether the position you indicate is actually the best tactical position for *Santa Fe* is a totally different issue, one of physics, time, distance, and the movements of the enemy. These are characteristics of the physical world and have nothing to do with trust.

QUESTIONS TO CONSIDER

- How would you counter any reluctance on the part of your team to have early, quick discussions with you, the boss, to make sure projects are on course?
- To what degree is trust present in your organization?
- Is your staff spending time and money creating flawless charts and reports that are, simultaneously, irrelevant?

- What can you do in your organization to add "a little rudder far from the rocks" to prevent needing "a lot of rudder next to the rocks"?
- What commonplace facts can you leverage to make information more valuable and accessible to your employees?
- Have you ever uncovered a "reason why" akin to Sled Dog's admission that the navigational chart legends depended on whatever color highlighter was at the ready?

"I Intend To . . ."

How proactive are senior managers and employees in your organization? Rewording our speech dramatically changed our level of proactivity.

January 21, 1999: Pearl Harbor, Hawaii
(159 days to deployment)

"Conn, maneuvering, reactor scram!" The reactor had just shut down. The engineer inserted the shutdown deliberately, testing his department's ability to find and repair a simulated fault.

The four days we had to regain our sea legs until we picked up Commodore Mark Kenny were jammed with training, qualification checkouts, strike exercises, and torpedo loading events. After picking up the inspection team, we would hunt for an enemy submarine heading toward Maui, where we'd shoot some exercise torpedoes against all the targets we were assigned. It would be fun, but I was nervous about how the ship would do. It was going to be our first big test.

"Inspection mentality" is a morale killer. This is the practice of focusing solely on the next inspection. While many ships gear their efforts toward doing well on the next inspection, on some ships this inspection mentality is so strong they refer to "ORSE patrols" and "TRE patrols." The Operational Reactor Safeguards Examination (ORSE) is a propulsion plant exam, and so they run predominantly engineering drills. The Tactical Readiness Evaluation (TRE) involves challenging navigation drills as well as shooting missiles and torpedoes, and so they run predominantly forward drills. On *Santa Fe*, doing well on inspections was going to be the natural outcome of being excellent, not the goal. Operational and tactical excellence and preparedness for service to the country were what mattered. If we were excellent and prepared, the drills and inspections would take care of themselves.

We were about to do a tactical inspection, so it was natural that the weapons officer (Weps), Lieutenant Dave Adams, had packed the schedule with weapons and tactical training. The engineer (Eng), Lieutenant Commander Rick Panlilio, wanted to do this engineering drill, and that seemed like a good idea to me because we needed to train both ends of the ship: the tactical end and the propulsion end. I'm glad I agreed to include such a drill because I learned a lesson of profound significance both to me and to the future of *Santa Fe*.

The drill was simple. The engineer would shut the reactor down with a simulated fault. The engineering department would troubleshoot to locate the problem, conduct the necessary repairs, and restart the reactor. While the reactor was shut down, we would have to shift propulsion from the large steam-powered main engines to a much smaller electric propulsion motor, called the EPM. The EPM can power the ship only at slow speed, but it's enough to get you home if the reactor is out of commission.

We set up for the drill. I was in the control room in the forward part of the submarine observing the officer of the deck and the ship control watch standers. In the engine room, Rick and his drill team set up and had started the drill by scramming (shutting down) the reactor.

The OOD was my senior department head, Lieutenant Commander Bill Greene, and he was doing all the right things. We had shifted propulsion from the main engines to an auxiliary electric motor, the EPM, to turn the propeller. The ship was coming shallow in order to use its diesel engine to provide electrical power and keep the battery charged until the reactor was restarted. During the long troubleshooting period while the nuclear electronics technicians were isolating the fault, I started to get bored. I fiddled with my flashlight, turning it on and off. Things were going too smoothly. I couldn't let the crew think their new captain was easy!

I nudged Bill and suggested we increase speed from "ahead one third" to "ahead two thirds" on the EPM to give the nuclear-trained enlisted men (nukes) more to worry about. This would significantly increase the rate of battery discharge and put pressure on the troubleshooters to find and correct the fault quickly. At "ahead two thirds," there is a near-continuous click-click-click on the battery amp-hour meter. An audible reminder that time is running out, it's physically unnerving!

"Ahead two thirds," he ordered.

Nothing happened.

The helmsman should have reached over and rung up ahead two thirds. Instead, I could see him squirming in his chair. No one said anything, and several awkward seconds passed. Astutely noting that the order hadn't been carried out, I asked the helmsman what was going on. He was facing his panel but reported over his shoulder, "Captain, there is no ahead two thirds on the EPM!"

Now, here's my excuse. As I've mentioned in an earlier chapter, I had not been on this class submarine before, and every ship I had been on previously had one third and two thirds on the EPM. I'm 100 percent sure that somewhere in being trained for my new submarine this fact had been covered, but it didn't stick amid the myriad technical details. I'd fallen back on what I'd known before.

I applauded the helmsman and grabbed Bill. In the corner of

the control room, I asked him if he knew there was no ahead two thirds on the EPM.

"Yes, Captain, I did."

"Well, why did you order it?" I asked, astounded.

"Because you told me to."

"What?"

"I thought you'd learned something secret at PCO school that they only tell the COs about."

He was being perfectly honest. By giving that order, I took the crew right back to the top-down, command-and-control leadership model. That my most senior, experienced OOD would repeat it was a giant wake-up call about the perils of that model for something as complicated as a submarine. What happens in a top-down culture when the leader is wrong? Everyone goes over the cliff. I vowed henceforth never to give an order, any order. I would let this be a lesson to myself to keep my mouth shut.

This incident brought to mind being chided as an OOD on my first submarine, the USS *Sunfish*, when I asked the captain for permission. "Just tell me what you are going to do!" he exclaimed. Thereafter, I started saying, "Captain, I intend to . . ." and he encouraged it.

That's what we decided to do on *Santa Fe*. It wasn't just when you were on watch, and it wasn't just for officers. It started filtering through the crew and permeating the way we did business. For my part, I would avoid giving orders. Officers would state their intentions with "I intend to . . ." and I would say, "Very well." Then each man would execute his plan.

Mechanism: Use "I Intend to . . ." to Turn Passive Followers into Active Leaders

"I INTEND TO . . ." was an incredibly powerful mechanism for CONTROL. Although it may seem like a minor trick of language, we found that it profoundly shifted ownership of the plan to the officers.

"I intend to . . ." didn't take long to catch on. The officers and crew loved it. I was the one who had a problem with it, ironically. I was worried that someone would say "I intend to . . ." when I was sleeping, and I would not be fully informed or understand what was happening. So, we made a rule that "I intend to . . ." only applied when I was awake. Other than that, it applied to everything.

A year later, I was standing on the bridge of the *Santa Fe* with Dr. Stephen Covey. He'd heard what we were doing and was interested in riding a submarine. Commodore Mark Kenny had been instrumental in arranging it. By this point, the crew had fully embraced our initiatives for control, and "I intend to . . ." was prominently visible. Throughout the day the officers approached me with "I intend to."

"Captain, I intend to submerge the ship. We are in water we own, water depth has been checked and is four hundred feet, all men are below, the ship is rigged for dive, and I've certified my watch team."

"Very well."

Dr. Covey was keenly interested in how the ship operated. I gave a copy of his book *The 7 Habits of Highly Effective People* to every chief and officer who reported aboard *Santa Fe*. We were applying many of the ideas in his book at an organizational level, to great success.

The Power of Words

The key to your team becoming more proactive rests in the language subordinates and superiors use. Here is a short list of "disempowered phrases" that passive followers use:

- Request permission to . . .
- I would like to . . .
- What should I do about . . .

- Do you think we should . . .
- Could we . . .

Here is a short list of "empowered phrases" that active doers use:

- I intend to . . .
- I plan on . . .
- I will . . .
- We will . . .

Interested readers will want to check out Stephen Covey's *The 8th Habit* for more ideas about the value of empowering language.

Then we extended the concept.

Frequently, I wouldn't just say, "Very well." There would be too many unanswered questions about the safety and appropriateness of the proposed event, so I found myself asking a bunch of questions.

One day I caught myself, and instead of asking the questions I had in mind, I asked the OOD what he thought I was thinking about his "I intend to submerge."

"Well, Captain, I think you are wondering if it's safe and appropriate to submerge."

"Correct. So why don't you just tell me why you think it is safe and appropriate to submerge. All I'll need to say is 'Very well.'"

Thereafter, the goal for the officers would be to give me a sufficiently complete report so that all I had to say was a simple approval. Initially, they would provide some information, but not all. Most of the time, however, they had the answers; they just hadn't vocalized them. Eventually, the officers outlined their complete thought processes and rationale for what they were about to do.

The benefit from this simple extension was that it caused them to think at the next higher level. The OODs needed to think like the captain, and so on down the chain of command. In effect, by articulating their intentions, the officers and crew were acting their way into the next higher level of command. We had no need of leadership development programs; the way we ran the ship *was* the leadership development program. One of the mechanisms I credit for the significantly disproportionate number of promotions that have been issued among *Santa Fe*'s officers and crew in the past decade was our "I intend to . . ." procedure.

Eventually we turned everything upside down. Instead of one captain giving orders to 134 men, we would have 135 independent, energetic, emotionally committed and engaged men thinking about what we needed to do and ways to do it right. This process turned them into active leaders as opposed to passive followers.

Later, I had the opportunity to talk with a friend of mine who had taught the PCO class. He was frustrated by the inability of too many officers in the training pipeline, who were almost ready to be promoted to commanding officers, to make decisions at the captain level. He said that these officers "came from good ships" but would become paralyzed when it came to decision making. I took issue with his categorizing them as "good ships." By using that term, he meant ships that didn't have problems—at least that we knew about. But this had obviously been accomplished using a top-down, leader-follower structure where the captain, when these officers were second in command, made the decisions. Moreover, it didn't appear that the captain had sufficiently involved or trained his XO.

This shows the degree to which we reward personality-centered leadership structures and accept their limitations. These may have been good ships, in that they avoided problems, but they certainly did not have good leadership.

Why did I say to the navigator that he should go ahead two thirds on the EPM? Being the captain of a nuclear-powered submarine can be a tremendous rush. You give orders, people jump, the reactor goes to higher power, the submarine surges through the water. You want more, you give more orders, and you become more controlling. It has a seductive pull on the leaders, but it is debilitating and energy sapping for the followers.

QUESTIONS TO CONSIDER

- What causes us to take control when we should be giving control?
- Can you recall a recent incident where your subordinate followed your order because he or she thought you had learned secret information "for executives only"?
- What would be the most challenging obstacle to implementing "I intend to . . ." in your place of business?
- Could your mid-level managers think through and defend their plan of action for the company's next big project?

Up Scope!

Do you like to help your people come to the right answers? I did, and that made matters worse.

January 27, 1999: Pearl Harbor, Hawaii
(153 days to deployment)

The chart table on a submarine gets to be a crowded spot. Lieutenant Dave Adams, Lieutenant Commander Bill Greene, and the XO were crowded around the chart table with me, along with Chief John Larson. We'd pushed Sled Dog, the quartermaster, out of the way.

Where was the enemy going? I scanned the chart and it came to me. I saw that they were likely heading for some congested waters near Maui.

"Here, we need to be *here* at 0600." I tapped the chart with the butt end of the flashlight at a spot in the Maui basin. If the enemy was indeed heading toward those congested waters, this location, upslope from them, looking into the deeper, quieter water, would be the spot from which we would launch our attack.

It was midnight. I was exhausted and needed a couple hours of sleep. We'd gone into Pearl Harbor and picked up Commodore Mark Kenny and his inspection team. The ship was doing well, but I felt I needed to be in too many places at once. For this, the overnight supervisors would have to drive *Santa Fe* into position: accounting for the movements of the enemy, the interfering maritime traffic, the wind and sea conditions, and a number of other factors.

I looked around. Heads nodded. Any questions? There were none. "Okay, call me if anything comes up that interferes with this plan or may make us want to reconsider it."

A more enlightened approach would have been to engage in a discussion about why I came up with the position and what assumptions were key to making that position work. That's what I wanted to do, but I just didn't have the energy or time anymore. All day, every day, it seemed like that's all I did. It was tiresome. I tried to stay as quiet as possible and let the officers run things with "I intend to . . ." but top-down was ingrained in how we operated and we fell back on bad habits.

January 28, 1999: On Board *Santa Fe* (152 days to deployment)

When I got up at 0500, I was dismayed to find that we were several miles out of position. Not only that, we were headed in the wrong direction, *away* from the enemy! Now the enemy was likely to be upslope of us! It would take several hours to reverse the situation, a tactical blunder that would result in a down check during an inspection but could spell death during combat. The watch team had allowed a series of short-term contacts and navigational issues to drive them rather than driving the ship to an optimal tactical position. We were still letting things happen to us rather than proactively making things happen.

Commodore Kenny was in the control room, observing our

team's interactions. I was exasperated but kept my cool. I realized the failure was mine. We weren't going to be able to go from top-down to bottom-up overnight.

My immediate reaction was to think that I needed to manage everything more carefully—"I should have checked at 0300"—but this would have put me back into the exact same situation I was in on board the *Will Rogers*. There needed to be a way out of this. Upon reflection, I decided that giving specific direction, as in my statement "We need to be *here* at 0600," without the under-lying thought processes just didn't work in the complex and unpredictable world we were in. There were no shortcuts. As the level of control is divested, it becomes more and more important that the team be aligned with the goal of the organization. At this point, although I'd talked about accomplishing our mission (a positive goal), the team was still in the old mind-set of avoiding problems (in this case, avoiding contacts to prevent counterdetec-tion and minimize the risk of collision). When it came to prose-cuting the enemy, a correct assessment of risk versus gain would have been more focused on driving the submarine to an optimal tactical position rather than avoiding contacts.

For the next several hours, we worked our way toward a better tactical position. We'd be making good progress, then have to turn back to avoid a fishing boat and lose ground. *Santa Fe* was operating at periscope depth (PD) in shallow water, so each turn took several minutes. It was slow going.

"Up scope." The OOD rolled the ring, and the hydraulics began lifting the periscope the eighteen feet to its fully raised position.

Santa Fe was just beneath the surface of the water. Even with the scope raised, a short pole of only about two feet would be vis-ible above the surface. Still, the ocean was quite smooth today and even at our slow speed our periscope could be visible. We'd raise the periscope for just a few seconds, rapidly look around, and lower it again.

We were in the final stages of a cat-and-mouse game with the enemy diesel submarine. The simulated war had escalated to the point where *Santa Fe* was authorized to sink it.

The enemy had picked this area deliberately. The shallow uneven bottom reduced the effectiveness of the torpedo, and to ensure a hit we would need a precise idea of the enemy's location. The best way to do this would be to actually see it, which is why we were at periscope depth, looking for the enemy sub visually. To accomplish this, we had packed more than twenty men into the control room, a space roughly half the area of a typical Starbucks.

We carried the Mk 48 ADCAP (advanced capability) torpedo. It is a devastating weapon against both surface ships and submarines. We launch the torpedo to intercept the target the way a hunter leads a duck. In addition, the torpedo has its own sonar system, looking for the target for a precise intercept. The torpedo streams a wire behind it that stays connected to the submarine, allowing us to see what the torpedo is seeing and redirect the torpedo, sending steering orders down the wire.

"Target!" Amid the buoys and haze, and against the Hawaiian Islands as a backdrop, the OOD saw the enemy's periscope and immediately lowered ours. If we could see him, he could see us.

"Captain, recommend firing point procedures!" Dave Adams was pushing me to order the attack and I liked that. As weapons officer, he knew we had all the pieces together for a successful shot: weapons loaded and ready in the tubes, an accurate bead on the target, and authorization to engage. Waiting for more precise information would only give the enemy more time to detect us.

"Very well, Weps." I wanted to acknowledge his initiative.

I ordered the attack. "Firing point procedures, submarine. Tube one primary, tube two backup."

I wiped the sweat off my brow.

The standard litany followed that order, as principal officer assistants reported readiness to launch. The next words I heard, however, were not part of that litany.

"Request to raise the BRA-34 to download the broadcast."

What? Raise the radio antenna?

We were at the end of our twelve-hour broadcast cycle. It was time to get our messages. We'd avoided raising this antenna because it sticks out of the water higher than the periscope and would need to remain up for several minutes, making detection of *Santa Fe* likely.

I resisted the urge to throw a fit. I glanced at Commodore Kenny, who was standing to the side of the control room. He was smiling as if they'd planned this wrinkle just to test me. Clearly, his radio inspector had been keeping him informed that we were approaching twelve hours on the broadcast and that the deadline to download our message traffic would likely come right at the worst time.

By pointing at the chart and giving my crew the solution, I had made things worse. I deprived them of the opportunity and obligation to think.

Tempted as I was to bark orders at this moment, I looked at my shoes instead. "We're not going to do that," I muttered. "We have to find another solution." Even if we lost the opportunity to attack right then, I needed to get everyone on board thinking.

I waited for several seconds. It worked.

The department heads jumped into a quick discussion. I resisted the urge to say anything, and stayed quiet. Seconds were ticking by and the uncertainties of the enemy's position were growing. Someone pointed out that if we sank the other ship we would have to report that by communicating, and when we did, we'd get the broadcast then. And oh, by the way, there'd be no one around to counterdetect us at that point!

"Captain, recommend continuing with the attack!"

Voilà!

"Final bearing and shoot!" The scope came up. This time I was on it. I pointed the scope on the enemy submarine and pushed the bearing button, sending the precise bearing to the computers calculating the intercept course.

"Set!" The bearing was entered; calculations were updated and sent to the torpedo.

"Shoot!" Dave Adams announced. By procedure, once I ordered "final bearing and shoot" the Weps ordered the final button push that launched the torpedo.

Woosh! We felt the shudder in the control room as high-pressure water rammed the ADCAP out of tube one, its motor started, and it was on its way.

"Unit running normally, wire good!"

"Unit has merged on the bearing of the target."

The normal reports were coming in.

Now we waited. Our torpedo would run out to where the enemy was and turn on. If all went well, it would see the target in its first couple of pings and home on in.

"Detect!" It saw the enemy. We checked our torpedo's location and where we thought the enemy was. We updated the enemy's position slightly.

"Acquire!" We had them!

"Loud explosion." (This was simulated by the inspector, who assessed that our torpedo had successfully attacked the enemy submarine.)

Cheers in the control room. We had achieved our first success!

Mechanism: Resist the Urge to Provide Solutions

I reflected on what had taken place and realized that as tired as I was, and despite the time it would have taken, I should have let my officers figure things out.

Emergency situations required snap decision making and clear orders. There's no time for a big discussion. Yet, the vast majority of situations do not require immediate decisions. You have time to let the team chew on it, but we still apply the crisis model of issuing rapid-fire orders. RESIST THE URGE TO PROVIDE SOLUTIONS is a mechanism for CONTROL. When you follow the leader-leader model, you must take time to let others react to the situation as well. You have to create a space for open decision by the entire team, even if that space is only a few minutes, or a few seconds, long. This is harder than in the leader-follower approach because it requires you to anticipate decisions and alert your team to the need for an upcoming one. In a top-down hierarchy, subordinates don't need to be thinking ahead because the boss will make a decision when needed.

This was a hard habit to break, both for my team and for me. Early in my command of the *Santa Fe*, we went to the training simulator where we practiced torpedo attacks. I had the fire control party with me, about thirty guys. I told them at the outset that I was not going to give any orders unless someone recommended it. We ended up driving in a straight line for thirty minutes because they all just thought I'd order the turn. It was painful.

How many times do issues that require decisions come up on short notice? If this is happening a lot, you have a reactive organization locked in a downward spiral. When issues aren't foreseen, the team doesn't get time to think about them; a quick decision by the boss is required, which doesn't train the team, and so on. No one has time to actually think through the issue.

You need to change that cycle. Here are a few ways to try to get your team thinking for themselves:

- If the decision needs to be made urgently, make it, then have the team "red-team" the decision and evaluate it.
- If the decision needs to be made reasonably soon, ask for team input, even briefly, then make the decision.
- If the decision can be delayed, then force the team to provide inputs. Do not force the team to come to consensus; that results in whitewashing differences and dissenting

votes. Cherish the dissension. If everyone thinks like you, you don't need them.

- How deeply is the top-down, leader-follower structure ingrained in how your business operates?
- Do you recognize situations in which you need to resist the urge to provide solutions?
- When problems occur, do you immediately think you just need to manage everything more carefully?
- What can you do at your next meeting with senior staff to create a space for open decision making by the entire team?

Who's Responsible?

Are you inadvertently sending a message that erodes ownership and responsibility among subordinates? We were.

January 28, 1999: On Board *Santa Fe*
(152 days to deployment)

In addition to observing the ship perform its tactical maneuvers, the inspection team also looks at administrative issues. In this case, they identified that *Santa Fe* had not responded to several messages we owed to higher authority—the squadron, Pacific Submarine Force (SUBPAC), and the maintenance facility. Naturally I wasn't happy, but I didn't want to shift too much attention away from the torpedo and missile shooting. After those events were over, however, I asked the XO about the missed items, and he brought out the "tickler" (add ominous music here), a three-inch binder maintained by his yeomen that had all of the messages—such as this one—that we received. They were sorted by department and due date. He looked in the book and proudly reported that, sure enough, we were tracking this particular message and knew we hadn't responded.

So we had a system that was focused on understanding the status instead of actually getting the work done. Unfortunately, everyone was too busy to look at the binder, and in any event, it was stuck up in a locker in the XO's stateroom. Like every other submarine we would have weekly "tickler" meetings where the department chiefs and department heads would sit in the wardroom for an hour or more going through the binder page by page. Of course, none of this activity actually resulted in getting any of the work done; it simply allowed us to catalogue what we were supposed to do and what we were delinquent on. It sucked up a lot of time, valuable supervisory time.

This was how everyone did it, always had.

There is no requirement to maintain a tickler, only a requirement to get the work done. What happened was that in the leader-follower structure that we teach, some commands long ago started keeping ticklers. Those ticklers then became seen as a useful tool for managing the work. The underlying message behind that method of doing business is not helpful; it's top-down, leader-follower, and it limits the authority, the initiative, the creativity, the job satisfaction, and ultimately the happiness of the team.

Fundamentally, this tickler process sends the following message: we will keep track and monitor you and your job performance. We will enforce (somehow) the proper performance of your job.

This erodes a more powerful message: you are responsible for your job.

The next tickler meeting was coming up and I invited myself.

I resisted the instinct to move into micromanagement mode. That would be moving in the wrong direction. How could we turn this on its head and reinforce the central tenet that the department heads, not the XO, were responsible for their departments?

We talked about how well the tickler had worked on other submarines and staffs that we'd worked on and with. Our experiences fell into several categories.

Some commands had a broken tickler and didn't get anything done. They didn't even know what they owed and were chronically late in completing tasking.

Other commands had a tickler and a sense of what they were missing, but they weren't efficiently getting the work done. This is the most inefficient because it has the lowest ratio of actual work accomplishment to effort. This was where we were.

Still other commands were "well run." They had a tickler, knew what was due, and got it done. This is moderately efficient because the work gets done, but there is still the overhead of maintaining the tickler and having those supervisory meetings.

We set out to invent an even more efficient way to do it, a new way.

Mechanism: Eliminate Top-Down Monitoring Systems

I reviewed the checking-out scenario, which was actually starting to work well. When checking out with the XO, the department heads were now telling him what they were doing, hadn't done, and needed help with. It was a bottom-up dialogue. Why couldn't we model our management of the tickler the same way?

The discussion went like this.

"Weps, who's responsible for your department?"

"I am, sir."

"Not the XO?"

"No."

"Then why should he spend time keeping a tickler for you and have you all sit in these agonizing tickler meetings?"

"He shouldn't."

"Okay. But here's the deal; you guys need to get the work done."

"We will." Chief David Steele reminded me that his department had worked through the night while we were in San Diego to get our VLS missile tubes 100 percent operational so we could participate in the battle group–wide Tomahawk missile exercise. What I didn't know was that Chief Steele had box seats at the Padres game (they came from behind to win) and had given those up. No one told him he had to do it or ordered him to do it. It was needed to support the mission and he just did it.

"Nav, do you remember when I was PCO sitting in the XO's stateroom and you 'checked out' with him?"

"Yes sir."

"Well, why was it the XO's job to tell you what you owed?"

"Well, I, uh, I don't know."

"It wasn't. So here's what we are going to do. You are all going to monitor your own departments and whatever is due. You are responsible, not me and not the XO, for getting it done."

And with that, we unburdened ourselves of the effort of maintaining the tickler. This had two advantages. First, it would be most efficient because the work would be getting done without the overhead of maintaining the tickler and those darned tickler meetings. Second, there would be no illusion about who was responsible for the performance of the various departments: the department heads were!

No one had ever seen this before, but we were going to give it a try.

ELIMINATING TOP-DOWN MONITORING SYSTEMS is a mechanism for CONTROL.

Sure, I was worried that a lot of stuff would slip through the cracks and *Santa Fe* would get a reputation for not getting the work done, but that didn't happen. I won't say that we never again received a message zinging us for not reporting something, but they were easily remedied and not that important. What was incredibly powerful was the idea that everyone was responsible for their own performance and the performance of their departments; that we weren't going to spend a lot of effort telling them what to do.

Supervisors frequently bemoan the "lack of ownership" in their employees. When I observe what they do and what practices they have in their organization, I can see how they defeat any attempt to build ownership.

Worse, if they've voiced their frustrations out loud, their employees perceive them as hypocritical and they lose credibility. Don't preach and hope for ownership; implement mechanisms that actually give ownership. Eliminating the tickler did that for us. Eliminating top-down monitoring systems will do it for you. I'm not talking about eliminating data collection and measuring processes that simply report conditions without judgment. Those are important as they "make the invisible visible." What you want to avoid are the systems whereby senior personnel are determining what junior personnel should be doing.

When it comes to processes, adherence to the process frequently becomes the objective, as opposed to achieving the objective that the process was put in place to achieve. The goal then becomes to avoid errors in the process, and when errors are made, additional overseers and inspectors are added. These overseers don't do anything to actually achieve the objective. They only identify when the process has gone bad after the fact.

In his book *Out of the Crisis*, W. Edwards Deming lays out the leadership principles that became known as TQL, or Total Quality Leadership. This had a big effect on me. It showed me how efforts to improve the process made the organization more efficient, while efforts to monitor the process made the organization less efficient. What I hadn't understood was the pernicious effect that "We are checking up on you" has on initiative, vitality, and passion until I saw it in action on *Santa Fe*.

TQL is now viewed as a passed fad. The Navy botched the introduction of TQL (done in a non-TQL way) so it's a bad word to many. That's too bad, because there are a lot of valuable ideas embedded in Deming's thinking. I recommend his writings to you.

QUESTIONS TO CONSIDER

- Are you underutilizing the ideas, creativity, and passion of your mid-level managers who want to be responsible for their department's work product?
- Can you turn over your counterpart to *Santa Fe*'s tickler to department heads and rid yourself of meetings in the process?
- How many top-down monitoring systems are in play within your organization?
- How can you eliminate them?

"A New Ship"

How comfortable are you with showing your gut feelings to your staff? We didn't even have the language to express doubt, ambiguity, or uncertainty.

January 29, 1999: En Route to Pearl Harbor
(151 days to deployment)

A submarine isn't designed to ride on top of an ocean's surface because the top of the sail, where the bridge is located, is only twenty feet above the water. On the bridge, you lack the periscope, sonar, contact, and geographic positioning displays you have in the control room, thirty feet below.

What you do have is a nice 360-degree view, something you don't have observing the world through the narrow lens of a periscope. So we drive the submarine from the bridge when on the surface. The only communication gear the driver has is a microphone into the submarine and a radio to talk to other ships. We came to augment this with a portable commercial radar we would rig up with a GPS display.

I was standing on top of the bridge in a harness. The inspection was essentially over and we were returning to port. Lieutenant Dave Adams was OOD, driving *Santa Fe* up the channel into Pearl Harbor. He chatted with the bridge phone talker and lookouts. Everyone, it seemed, was in a buoyant mood except me. We had followed the attack on the submarine with a successful attack on an enemy surface ship. We sank two "enemy" vessels, shooting two for two, and hadn't been counterdetected. We had operated *Santa Fe* safely and effectively. We'd done well.

Still, I was thinking about how the inspection had gone in more critical terms and how much I'd had to drive solutions to problems.

"Bridge, navigator. Mark the turn." I overheard Lieutenant Commander Bill Greene's voice on the bridge loudspeaker. The navigation team in the control room was using bearings from the periscope and GPS to determine where *Santa Fe* was in the channel and when we needed to turn.

"Nav, bridge, aye," Dave acknowledged, holding the microphone to his mouth, but he didn't order the turn. I waited a second.

"Weps, are you going to turn?" I asked directly. In the narrow channel, every second counted. I glanced sideways at the familiar day markers and palm trees and knew we were at the point where we needed to turn.

"Yes, three seconds. I thought they were early." He seemed miffed I had prodded him.

"Helm, right fifteen degrees rudder." *Santa Fe* started a slow turn to the right, lining up with the next leg of the channel. It worked out just fine.

But I could see Dave had lost initiative, lost confidence, and lost control. He was no longer driving the submarine, I was. His job satisfaction had just taken a big hit.

Thinking Out Loud

Once we were safely moored at the pier, I pondered what had happened during our two days at sea: mispositioning the ship despite my explicit instructions; the inappropriate and surprising request to raise the communications mast in the middle of the attack; my interfering when Dave was driving the ship into port without my knowing what he was thinking. On top of all that, only about 10 percent of the crew were actually practicing the "three-name" greeting. Because we were in the middle of an inspection, I'd said nothing. As much as I had vowed not to give orders and to let an empowered group of officers "intend" the way to victory, I found myself on too many occasions running to the control room, or torpedo room, or sonar room, to solve some crisis and set things right. The successes we'd had still relied too much on my personal involvement. I wanted to be able to have a heart attack and have the ship continue to effectively take the fight to the enemy.

Why did these things happen? How did we get here?

While we waited for the inspection team to finish their report, I discussed these problems with the remaining department heads. We came up with several causes.

First, the crew had lost perspective about what was important. My guys assured me that "during a real war" it would never happen, but I wasn't so sure. The Navy's experience at the beginning of World War II was that too many submarine crews and captains took their peacetime practices into war with them. The result was overly cautious operations that failed to inflict significant damage on the enemy. To me this was another manifestation of a lack of organizational clarity, and a tendency to avoid mistakes rather than achieve excellence.

Second, there was an absence of informal communication. There had been no "in an hour we will need to download the broadcast" and "the broadcast is coming down in five minutes," which would have kept the issue front and center. We were our own worst enemy here.

As naval officers, we stress formal communications and even have a book, the *Interior Communications Manual*, that specifies exactly how equipment, watch stations, and evolutions are spoken, written, and abbreviated. By consistently using these terms, we avoid confusion. For example, we *shut* valves, we don't *close* them, because "close" could be confused with "blow." We *prepare* to snorkel, but then we report being *ready*—not *prepared*—to snorkel.

This adherence to formal communications unfortunately crowds out the less formal but highly important contextual information needed for peak team performance. Words like "I think . . ." or "I am assuming . . ." or "It is likely . . ." that are not specific and concise orders get written up by inspection teams as examples of informal communications, a big no-no. But that is just the communication we need to make leader-leader work.

We also discussed what had happened on the bridge as we approached Pearl Harbor. Here's what I wish Dave had been saying: "Captain, the navigator has been marking the turns early. I am planning on waiting five seconds, then ordering the turn," or "I'm seeing the current running past this buoy pretty strongly and I'm going to turn early because of it." Now the captain can let the scene play out. The OOD retains control of his job, his initiative; he learns more and becomes a more effective officer. He's driving the submarine! He loves his job and stays in the Navy.

We called this "thinking out loud."

We worked hard on this issue of communication. It was for everyone. I would think out loud when I'd say, in general, here's where we need to be, and here's why. They would think out loud with worries, concerns, and thoughts. It's not what we picture when we think of the movie image of the charismatic and confident leader, but it creates a much more resilient system. Later, even though *Santa Fe* was performing at the top of the fleet, officers steeped in the leader-follower mind-set would criticize what they viewed as the informal communications on *Santa Fe*. If you limit all discussion to crisp orders and eliminate all contextual discussion, you get a pretty quiet control room. That was viewed as good. We cultivated the opposite approach and encouraged a constant buzz of discussions among the watch officers and crew. By monitoring that level of buzz, more than the actual content, I got a good gauge of how well the ship was running and whether everyone was sharing information.

Inspection Debrief

"SUBRON Seven, arriving." Commodore Mark Kenny was back on board to do the inspection debrief. If the grades had been bad he would have called me up to his office in Building 660. Nevertheless, I was apprehensive about our grades. I desperately wanted a win for the crew to build on.

"David, congratulations. *Santa Fe* is a new ship. You and your crew earned an above average." I was stunned. In the submarine force, an "above average" actually is above the mathematical average for the fleet.

"My staff is very impressed," the commodore continued. "They've been telling me all week how sailors have been welcoming them to *Santa Fe*, asking questions, being curious, and taking initiative. I was worried about the situations where your team let you down, and you handled those well."

We were both thinking back to my behavior during PCO operations when I stepped over a fellow PCO to get the job done. Neither of us needed to mention it.

I grabbed the loudspeaker (1MC) and broadcast to the ship the great news. I could hear the men cheering. I cited specific examples of enthusiasm, initiative, and technical competence among the crew. The officers were congratulated on their enthusiasm and the initiative demonstrated throughout the command. All were smiles. Along with Chiefs in Charge and our nascent "I intend to . . . ," the 10 percent of the crew who practiced the three-name rule were enough to create a major change in impression.

This affirmation brought us important credibility and served as a sturdy foundation for the changes we wanted to make going forward. Turns out we were going to need it.

The good times lasted less than an hour.

Mechanism: Think Out Loud

THINK OUT LOUD is a mechanism for CONTROL because when I heard what my watch officers were thinking, it made it much easier for me to keep my mouth shut and let them execute their plans. It was generally when they were quiet and I didn't know what they would do next that I was tempted to step in. Thinking out loud is essential for making the leap from leader-follower to leader-leader.

Later, when I was the head of the tactical inspection team for two years, I rode most of the submarines in the Pacific. I can tell you that forward or aft, attack submarine or ballistic missile submarine, there is a tremendous reluctance for the junior officers to tell their superiors anything other than 100 percent certified information. There's no room in our military language and no pictures in our heads for the kinds of context-rich conversations that are critical to good team performance. We aren't comfortable talking about hunches or gut feelings or anything with probabilities attached to it.

Santa Fe was no exception. There was a strong cultural bias against thinking out loud. In the hierarchical structure I inherited, there wasn't much need for it, and the language for thinking out loud hadn't been exercised. We worked hard to ingrain this informal yet informative manner of speaking into the crew, and then along came a new sailor straight from school, and he wouldn't want to say anything. I often wondered why we aren't naturally learning the most effective way to communicate as a team. We say submarining is a team sport, but in practice it often amounts to a bunch of individuals, each working in his own shell, rather than a rich collaboration.

So, in order to make the fewest mistakes when reporting on things, we say as little as possible. This is a problem throughout the submarine force, and we worked hard to encourage the entire crew to say what they saw, thought, believed, were skeptical about, feared, worried about, and hoped for the future. In other words, all the things that don't show up in the *Interior Communications Manual*. We realized we didn't even have a language with which to express uncertainty and we needed to build that.

THINK OUT LOUD also works as a mechanism for ORGANIZATIONAL CLARITY. If all you need your people to do is follow orders, it isn't important that they understand what you are trying to accomplish. But we operate in a highly complex world, with the vagaries of an ever-changing environment and the opposition of a diligent and patient enemy. It's not enough to put a finger on the chart and hope things come out well.

When I, as the captain, would "think out loud," I was in essence imparting important context and experience to my subordinates. I was also modeling that lack of certainty is strength and certainty is arrogance.

QUESTIONS TO CONSIDER

- Do you ever walk around your facility listening solely to what is being communicated through informal language?
- How comfortable are people in your organization with talking about their hunches and their gut feelings?

- How can you create an environment in which men and women freely express their uncertainties and fears as well as their innovative ideas and hopes?
- Are you willing to let your staff see that your lack of certainty is strength and certainty is arrogance?
- To what degree does trust factor in the above?

"We Have a Problem"

Who are your company's inspectors, and how can you use them to best advantage? An approach of embracing external organizations helped *Santa Fe* retain control of our destiny.

January 29, 1999: In Port, Pearl Harbor
(151 days to deployment)

"Captain, I intend to bring on shore power and shut down the reactor."

"Very well, Eng." Lieutenant Commander Rick Panlilio had quickly embraced our "I intend to . . ." approach and was off and running. When the ship came into port, we would hook up to shore power through four massive cables powered from a pier bunker supplying 440-volt electricity. Then we could shut down the reactor.

In order to safely execute this, and many other evolutions, we hung red danger tags on breakers, valves, or switches that, if operated during the procedure, would endanger someone's life.

These red tags are held inviolate, and any violation of the system is heavily scrutinized.

The tags would be hung first so that while the crew were connecting the four cables those cables were not inadvertently energized. This would be an electrical shock hazard to personnel as well as an equipment damage hazard because the submarine and pier electrical systems needed to be deliberately synchronized before being connected. This was a common routine, something we did every time *Santa Fe* returned from sea.

I was walking the ship thanking the crew for their hard work on the inspection. It was a big shot in the arm to do so well, and morale, for the moment, was high. As soon as I saw Rick, I knew something was wrong. The engineer was approaching with a cloud over his face.

"We had a problem with shore power. We violated a red tag."

Ugh. My heart sank. Anything but shore power, I thought. *Santa Fe* was under scrutiny for previous maintenance and procedural mistakes, some of which had been with shore power. Continued problems with shore power would indicate that we hadn't moved beyond poor past practices.

In this case, a sailor had energized breakers on the pier after the conditions for energizing them had been met (so there was no hazard), but he hadn't cleared the red tag before doing so (indicating we were just lucky). You don't want to be accidentally safe.

While I was directly and immediately accountable to Submarine Squadron Seven, and Commodore Mark Kenny, for the performance of *Santa Fe*, I was also accountable to Naval Reactors for the safe operation of the reactor plant. Naval Reactors is the organization set up by Admiral Hyman Rickover to build, maintain, manage, man, and certify naval nuclear power operations. It has an incredible record of success as a result of well-thought-out management processes. One of the reasons for success is that each port has an independent Naval Reactors team that reports back through a special chain of command directly to the director, a four-star admiral.

To understand the importance of this, recall the Enron–Arthur Andersen scandal. When Enron imploded in 2001, Arthur Andersen, the auditor, was earning $25 million annually from audit fees and an additional $25 million from consulting fees. They were inspectors and performers. Human instinct gets in the way of adequate inspection and enforcement when an individual or a group is also responsible for correcting deficiencies in performance. The Naval Reactors local field representatives are structured in a way that would make such conflicts of interest impossible. They are chartered to ensure safe reactor plant operations, period. They are freed of the burden of worrying about how hard things are, what the effect will be on retention of another Saturday training session, or how a delayed underway will impact the operational commander. This independence frequently aggravates ship drivers like me because Naval Reactors appears to be obstructionist, but they play a critically important role. It's one of the reasons for the long-term success of the program.

No one was hurt. Nevertheless, the engineer said he would report the problem up the chain, to both Squadron Seven and Naval Reactors. Ugh again. There was guidance on what kind of problems should be reported to which organization. This seemed to fall on the border, and I was tempted to handle it "in-house." Why did we need all this outside attention just as things were starting to go well? My instincts were to somehow protect my people from the scrutiny of these outside organizations. We could have not reported it; they would likely have never known. On the other hand, reporting it would invite additional monitor watches, possibly additional periodic and one-time reports, skepticism about the competency of *Santa Fe*'s leadership, and a lot of management time.

Rick was adamant, and he was right. We set up a critique for the next day, Saturday, and he called his counterparts at Squadron Seven and the Naval Reactors office and invited them to the critique. I called Commodore Kenny and told him as well. I fought off any thought of trying to let our problem slide by and openly welcomed the oversight organizations into our tent.

We called this idea of being open and inviting outside criticism "Embrace the inspectors."

Even so, Saturday was going to be a long day.

Mechanism: Embrace the Inspectors

We applied "embrace the inspectors" not only to one-time critiques and problems such as the shore power mishap, but also to entire inspections. We would utilize the inspectors to disseminate our ideas throughout the squadron, to learn from others, and to document issues to improve the ship.

This mechanism sends the signal that we are in charge of our destiny, not controlled by some force. It runs counter to the instincts expressed by many of my officers and chiefs to minimize the ship's visibility to the outside, especially when problems were involved. EMBRACE THE INSPECTORS is a mechanism for CONTROL, organizational control. In other words, the crew of *Santa Fe* are responsible for *Santa Fe*. We found we needed this parallelism with internal control. Later, we'd hand out T-shirts that jokingly read, "DON'T BE A VICTIM."

Concerning areas where we were doing something exceptionally innovative or expertly, we viewed the inspectors as advocates to share our good practices with. Concerning areas where we were doing things poorly and needed help, we viewed them as sources of information and solutions. This created an atmosphere of learning and curiosity among the crew, as opposed to an attitude of defensiveness.

Later on in my command, *Santa Fe* had a material inspection by a group of officers from the Board of Inspection and Survey (INSURV). Their reports carry significant weight and expose the submarine force to "big Navy" observers. Officers have lost their commands over bad INSURV inspections. When the INSURV team reported to our submarine, I handed them a list of known deficiencies. These were things that were so fundamental to the design or so difficult to repair that we had been unsuccessful. By getting them documented in the INSURV report, we ensured that the Navy would apply resources to fixing the problems, thus making all submarines more effective warships.

Embrace the inspectors turned out to be an incredibly powerful vehicle for learning. Whenever an inspection team was on board, I would hear crew members saying things like, "I've been having a problem with this. What have you seen other ships do to solve it?" Most inspection teams found this attitude remarkable.

As a result, *Santa Fe* was getting superior grades on inspections. Over time our sailors learned a lot and became incredibly good at their jobs; they also continued to evince a hunger for learning.

Embrace the inspectors can be viewed as a mechanism to enhance competence, but I think it fits even better in the discussion of control because it allowed us not only to be better submariners but also to maintain control of our destiny.

QUESTIONS TO CONSIDER

- How do you use outside groups, the public, social media comments, and government audits to improve your organization?
- What is the cost of being open about problems in your organization and what are the benefits?

- How can you leverage the knowledge of those inspectors to make your team smarter?
- How can you improve your team's cooperation with those inspectors?
- How can you "use" the inspectors to help your organization?

PART III

COMPETENCE

One of the two pillars that support control is competence. Competence means that people are technically competent to make the decisions they make. On a submarine, it means having a specific technical understanding of physics, electricity, sound in water, metallurgy, and so on.

The emphasis in the book thus far has been on pushing decision making and control to lower and lower levels in the organization. We found, however, that control by itself wasn't enough. The chapters in this part will focus on the mechanisms we employed to strengthen technical competence. They are:

- Take deliberate action.
- We learn (everywhere, all the time).
- Don't brief, certify.
- Continually and consistently repeat the message.
- Specify goals, not methods.

16

"Mistakes Just Happen!"

Are you content with the reason "Well, mistakes just happen" when it comes to managing your business? We rejected the inevitability of mistakes and came up with a way to reduce them.

January 30, 1999: In Port, Pearl Harbor
(150 days to deployment)

Saturday morning and the wardroom of the USS *Santa Fe* was packed. The petty officer who had caused the red tag violation, members of our watch team, the engineering officer of the watch, the engineer (Lieutenant Commander Rick Panlilio), the XO, the division officer, the COB, and the senior nuclear chief (Chief Brad Jensen) were sitting around the table. In addition, we had the observers from Squadron Seven and Naval Reactors.

I sat at the head of the table with the flashlight in front of me, thinking about how to approach this critique. It wasn't going to be good enough to just have a bunch of empowered people; we needed actually to be better.

The petty officer involved was a well-intentioned sailor who'd never been in trouble. I was sympathetic to the crew, who had worked incredibly hard over the past two weeks to get the ship under way, conduct our training, do the inspection, and accommodate all the changes. This was something I would wrestle with my entire command tour—balancing the courage to hold people accountable for their actions with my compassion for their honest efforts. We would need to understand what had happened, and I didn't want to take the easy way out and blame the petty officer who had moved the tag in error.

One measure of discipline in a military unit is the number of captain's mast cases. Captain's mast, also known as nonjudicial punishment (NJP), is a form of military justice that allows the captain to invoke near-immediate punishment without a trial by court-martial. Punishments are classified as administrative and are limited generally to forfeiture of pay, reduction in rank, or restriction to the boat. On board *Santa Fe*, there had been a couple captain's masts a month and that was too many.

It was widely assumed that if you violated a red tag you would go to captain's mast. The idea was to convey that this was important business and you had to pay attention. While that was true, I didn't believe in invoking a captain's mast automatically.

Eventually my department heads and chiefs would lead critiques, but I needed to lead this one. When I opened the meeting, no one—least of all me—expected to be there for eight hours.

"Let me start by welcoming the squadron and Naval Reactors representatives."

Several documents lay before us on the table: the procedure, a watch bill, and the tags themselves, among others. Later on during my command we would end up with a finely honed approach to conducting these critiques, but at this point, it was a bit ad hoc. We were developing the methodology as we went along. (To see where we ended up, and for a more detailed process for conducting critiques, visit davidmarquet.com to read "How we learn from our mistakes on nuclear submarines: A seven-step process.")

I opened the proceedings.

"Petty Officer M, can you tell me what happened?"

"Well, I knew we met conditions to shut the breaker, and I was just thinking that was the next step in the procedure. We had the procedure out and had reviewed it. I knew the red tags were hanging but just moved them aside to shut the breaker. Not sure what I was thinking."

Gasps.

"You moved a red tag aside?"

"Yes, it was hanging right in front of the breaker. There was one on each of the three pier breakers, three across, right there."

Murmuring.

I'm sure he was expecting to go to captain's mast and be fined. Yet, he was willing to tell us the truth quite bluntly without any attempt at obfuscation. This needed to be rewarded.

"Thank you very much for your candor. You and the rest of the watch team can go home. Supervisors stay behind."

This caused a stir. What, no recriminations? No captain's mast? No yelling?

I was taking a risk. If we later discovered that someone's actions were sufficiently neglectful to warrant punishment I would have painted myself into a box. However, I felt the candor and honesty of Petty Officer M were more important than continuing the current process of inquisition, fear, and punishment.

"Now, gentlemen, how are we going to prevent this from happening again?"

And that's what we spent the next seven and a half hours talking about.

Mechanism: Take Deliberate Action

We ran through all the usual suspects. First, it was suggested that we do some refresher training, a commonly proposed solution.

"Let me ask you this. Training implies a knowledge deficiency. I should be able to identify that with a test. So what question on a test do you think any of these guys would have gotten wrong?" No one could think of one. It wasn't a knowledge deficiency, and training wasn't the solution.

"We need to add supervision." This is another favorite solution, like adding the XO to the chart review process. We discussed what a supervisor would do, where he would stand, and how he could have prevented this mistake. Grudgingly, it was agreed that adding a supervisor might have prevented shutting down the second and third breakers, but not the first. Anyway, we already had significant supervision of the event through the Chief in Charge, the watch officer, the electrical division officer, and the engineer. If all those supervisors hadn't prevented it from happening, how would adding another one help? No one could think of the mechanism by which an additional supervisor would have prevented the mistake.

I pushed the team to come up with something that would have prevented the mistake in the first place. Exasperated with my unwillingness to accept any of the rote answers, someone blurted out, "Captain, mistakes just happen!"

Now we were getting somewhere. We discussed what it would take to reduce mistakes made at the deck plate level, at the interface between the operators and the equipment, not simply discover them afterward. These were mistakes such as turning the wrong valve, opening the wrong breaker, and moving red tags—actions no one consciously meant to do.

"Sir, it's attention to detail." This was a commonly used phrase as well, but telling the men to pay more attention didn't seem likely to make a difference in the long run in the number of mistakes. We'd tried that before.

"How so?"

"Well, he was just in auto. He didn't engage his brain before he did what he did; he was just executing a procedure."

I thought that was perceptive. We discussed a mechanism for engaging your brain before acting. We decided that when operating a nuclear-powered submarine we wanted people to act deliberately, and we decided on "take deliberate action" as our mechanism. This meant that prior to any action, the operator paused and vocalized and gestured toward what he was about to do, and only after taking a deliberate pause would he execute the action. Our intent was to eliminate those "automatic" mistakes. Since the goal of "take deliberate action" was to introduce deliberateness in the mind of the operator, it didn't matter whether anyone was around or not. Deliberate actions were not performed for the benefit of an observer or an inspector. They weren't for show.

Our mechanism to prevent recurrence of the problem was to implement the taking of deliberate actions on board *Santa Fe*. I would take no punitive action against the honest petty officer who had pushed aside the red tag. The Squadron Seven and Naval Reactors observers would go back and brief their supervisors on our plan, and they would make an assessment of *Santa Fe* and me. Since deliberate action seemed like a useful concept and I was a new captain, I figured they would withhold judgment and just see how it played out. That's what I was banking on, at any rate, because we needed more time to implement the changes that would make the sub and its crew excellent.

On Monday we had quarters on the pier to discuss the concept "take deliberate action" with the crew. I first explained what had happened with the red tag and the critique of the incident, and then I described what thinking deliberately meant and why we were going to do it. Even though it wasn't presented as a bargain, I think that the crew, knowing their shipmate had been spared captain's mast, were more receptive to the alternative—take deliberate action.

Deliberate action was accepted by the nuclear-trained personnel fairly readily because it built on a concept they had been exposed to at nuclear power school called "point and shoot." Unfortunately, deliberate action was a tough sell with much of the rest of the crew, and we would ultimately pay for that.

Deliberate Action Is Not for Show

I believe "take deliberate action" was the single most powerful mechanism that we implemented for reducing mistakes and making *Santa Fe* operationally excellent. It worked at the interface between man and machine: where petty officers were touching the valves, pumps, and switches that made the submarine and its weapons systems work. TAKE DELIBERATE ACTION is a mechanism for COMPETENCE. But selling the crew on this mechanism's value was hard going.

One problem in getting the crew to perform deliberately was the perception that deliberate action was for someone else's (a supervisor's, an inspector's) benefit. Even though we continually talked about how deliberate action was to prevent the individual from making silly mistakes, I would overhear sailors discussing deliberate action among themselves in this misperceived way.

The second problem was overcoming the perception that deliberate action was something you did as a training exercise, but in a "real situation," you would just move your hands as fast as possible. I used the following thought experiment to dispel this error: Suppose we are conducting a training drill around Pearl Harbor and the ship loses all propulsion due to errors. What happens? We would surface and call for help, which is nearby. We'd critique the event and write the appropriate reports. No one would die. What happens, however, if we lose all propulsion in a "real situation" in the face of the enemy due to errors? Now people might die. The key is that as the importance of doing things right increases, so does the need to act deliberately.

How Can You Implement Deliberate Action?

If you are in a business where there is an interface between humans and nature, the concept of taking deliberate action is pretty clear-cut. Electrical utilities, airlines and cruise lines, manufacturing plants, and hospitals are examples. In these kinds of organizations, you'll be able to see immediately how acting deliberately would help reduce mistakes. The challenge will be when things are happening quickly, or need to happen quickly, as in a casualty in a power plant or emergency room procedures in a hospital. It's even more important that actions be performed correctly then. You don't have time to "undo" something that's wrong.

If your business doesn't have an obvious interface with nature and is more service or intellectual, take deliberate action still applies, but in a slightly different way. It applies at the moment someone signs a form, authorizes an action, or enters a keystroke.

We didn't realize it at the time, but it turned out that take deliberate action had two tremendous benefits in addition to reducing errors. Rather, as a mechanism to reduce errors, it operated in two additional ways.

First, in team settings, when operators paused and vocalized and gestured, it allowed adjacent operators to step in and correct mistaken actions before they were taken. When I arrived at *Santa Fe*, many operators felt it was a point of prowess to operate as quickly as possible, and we had to overcome this. For example, the reactor operator in a pump shift may say, "Shifting number one reactor coolant pump to fast," and he would be pulling the switch at the same time he said the word *fast*. Unfortunately, if he accidentally had his hand on the switch for pump number two, it would be too late to stop him, and the wrong pump would be shifted. In exercising caution and deliberateness, the pause prior to starting the pump would allow the operator sitting next to him to stop him or for him to recognize the error himself.

In addition, when we ran drills, we would station monitors whose job it was to intervene to prevent inappropriate action. The drill monitor would have full insight into the drill and would know which actions were allowable and which ones were not. If the operator was tempted to take an inappropriate action, either intentionally or not, the monitor would stop him. Unfortunately, with the operators moving quickly, the monitors frequently only recorded errors after they happened because they didn't have a chance to intervene. This was especially true if the operator announced the correct action but became confused in the stress of trying to respond properly to a casualty and physically operated the wrong switch, breaker, or valve.

Later, when *Santa Fe* earned the highest grade on our reactor operations inspection that anyone had seen, the senior inspector told me this: "Your guys made the same mistakes—no, your guys *tried* to make the same number of mistakes—as everyone else. But the mistakes never happened because of deliberate action. Either they were corrected by the operator himself or by a teammate."

He was describing a resilient organization, one where error propagation is stopped.

Eventually we would expand deliberate action to administrative paperwork. When documents were signed carelessly, we injected the concept of deliberate action into the act (mostly for officers) of signing papers and authorizing events.

Many people talk about teamwork but don't develop mechanisms to actually implement it. Taking deliberate action is certainly one.

If your company is operating a power plant or is manufacturing tools, it's easy to see how you could apply deliberate action. But what if you are trading bonds, operating a hospital, or engaged in a service industry?

I think deliberate action still applies. In more administrative actions, we applied take deliberate action to the moment of signing the form authorizing an action. We wanted that signature to be deliberate. Recently, the case of the robo-signing in bank foreclosures demonstrates an excellent counterexample, but even in normal cases, I've seen where large stacks of administrative paperwork are just signed off on without much thought. Applied broadly, that will eventually get you into trouble.

QUESTIONS TO CONSIDER

- How do you react when an employee admits to doing something on autopilot, without deliberately thinking about the action or its consequences?
- Do you think that by implementing a system of taking deliberate action you can eliminate errors in your company, or within certain departments in your company?
- Will employees in your workplace revert to acting hastily and automatically in a real-life situation?
- How effectively do you learn from mistakes?

17

"We Learn"

Have you tried to divest control without first making sure your organization is competent to handle more decision-making authority? I learned the hard way that control without competence is chaos.

February 13, 1999: Makalapa Housing Area, Pearl Harbor, Hawaii
(136 days to deployment)

I was just getting back from a run around the Makalapa housing area where we lived in Pearl Harbor, letting my mind wander over my first month in command, when I had an insight. I was thinking about another problem we had shortly after the shore power incident. This time the problem occurred in the torpedo room. An inappropriate valve operation removed hydraulics from a torpedo handling mechanism, which resulted in its moving out of position. While deliberate action would have helped, the issue here was more one of technical competence. The guys doing the work just didn't understand the necessary system interconnections and responses.

Unlike the problem with shore power, it was difficult to understand what actually happened with the torpedo room problem. This was a weapons department issue, and Lieutenant Dave Adams had the responsibility to figure it out. We gathered logs, procedures, and records. We interviewed the participants. Who gave what orders? What procedure were you following? Who was the required conventional weapons handling supervisor for this evolution? The answers were vague and evasive. Moreover, when Dave probed the level of knowledge with questions like "What happens if you turn this valve with this part of the system depressurized?" the guys didn't do well.

After the problem occurred, I was unsure we were on the right path. I went to see Commodore Mark Kenny.

"I'm questioning my approach," I began. "Things just don't seem to be getting that much better fast enough. Just when I think we've got things going in the right direction, something like this happens."

"Look, I'm not surprised. I figured things would get worse before they got better. Right now you've got the space to make the changes you are making. I'll keep everyone else off your back. You only need to worry about me, and I think you're on the right track," the commodore assured me. I was glad because not everyone on the waterfront was rooting for us. There were twenty submarines stationed in Pearl Harbor, and though some of those captains were starting to come by to learn what we were doing, rumor was there was another group that would have been just as happy if our little experiment fell on its face.

We had been taking actions that pushed authority down the chain of command, that empowered the officers, chiefs, and crew, but the insight that came to me was that as authority is delegated, technical knowledge at all levels takes on a greater importance. There is an extra burden for technical competence.

If all you need to do is what you are told, then you don't need to understand your craft. However, as your ability to make decisions increases, then you need intimate technical knowledge on which to base those decisions. The laws of nature govern a submarine, and those laws are uncaring. With physics, you don't have problems; you only have the consequences of your actions. They become problems when we decide that what happened wasn't what we wanted to happen.

This was going to be hard. We were going to have to train our guys to a higher level of technical competence if we wanted to give them more authority. Fundamentally, this is where I think I failed on the *Will Rogers*. I had tried to push authority and control, but the technical competence of the engineering department, who were accustomed to being given specific guidance, had atrophied. It wasn't up to the level sufficient for making the decisions I had been pushing to them. I had assumed the requisite level of technical competence and I hadn't taken the necessary steps. Control without competence is chaos.

At times like this, I felt an impulse to just say screw it, it's not worth it, let's just go back to the leader-follower model. That will save me a lot of time and trouble in training. However, with Commodore Kenny's support, I was determined to persist. I decided to double down on our efforts.

This thought process helped me with another project we'd been working on: codifying our core principles into a creed and set of command principles. To get to our creed, I wanted something so basic that it would be applicable to every member of the crew every day.

During discussions with the officers and chiefs, we discussed what we did. Their answers were too vague at first:

- We supervise.
- We enforce standards.
- We schedule.
- We prepare for war.

We tried getting more specific, but now their answers were too much so:

- We operate systems of the submarine, preparing to engage in combat operations if called upon.
- We walk around and observe system performance and people's operations.
- We make decisions about how to best employ *Santa Fe*.
- We load torpedoes, determine enemy location, and program the torpedoes to attack the enemy.

We talked about this again. With the perspective of needing to increase technical competence in mind, we thought about the simple reality "we learn," and that's what we adopted. It was something that every member of the crew did every day. It seemed to be the basic element that unified all of our actions.

No matter what we were doing, we would figure out how to extract the maximum learning from that event. Our philosophy was that we just didn't have time to add a bunch of lectures, but the submarine gave us hundreds of opportunities a day to learn. Once we started looking for those learning opportunities, we found them everywhere.

We ended up codifying the philosophy of "we learn" with a statement of our creed.

USS *Santa Fe* Creed

What do we do on a day-to-day basis?
    We learn.

Why is "learning" a better word than "training"?
    Training implies passivity; it is done to us. We are trained;
    we attend training. Learning is active; it is something
    we do.

What do we learn?

We learn how to prepare a submarine for success in combat.

Why would we need to go to combat?

We would go to combat if called upon by our country to defend the Constitution of the United States.

Why is that important?

The personal liberty, well-being, and economic prosperity we enjoy in the United States are unique throughout the history of mankind. Man's life has generally been short, hard, and brutish. The democratic system we have and the importance of individual rights specified by the Constitution are the reasons for our emotional and physical prosperity. It's an important document, worthy of being defended. You are not alone in deciding this, as many have died defending the Constitution before you.

Why submarines?

Submarines can accomplish unique missions no other platform can accomplish. The American submarine force has a tremendous heritage of defending democracy. For example, during World War II, the submarine force, while only making up 2 percent of the Navy, sank over 50 percent of all Japanese vessels sunk. This was a critical contribution to winning that war.

If all we do is learn, how does the work get done?

We do the work. But, we learn by doing—maintenance, evolutions, casualty drills, studying. So, when we are working, even doing field day, we are learning.

It seems like a trick; we're still doing the same thing, we're just calling it something different.

Yes and no. Yes, in that we will still keep the boat clean, drill, do maintenance, qualify, and the myriad other tasks that take up our time. No, in that how you look at things makes a difference. Instead of looking at a task as just a chore, look at it as an opportunity to learn more about the associated piece of equipment, the procedure, or if nothing else, about how to delegate or accomplish tasks.

How does the training program fit in?

The training program is a part of the learning process, but by no means all of it. Training is a subset of learning, which in turn is a subset of personal growth. We strive to grow each day.

Therefore, our vision of our command is a learning and competence factory.

The raw materials are the new personnel reporting aboard each week, new equipment, and tactics. The product is well-qualified, experienced sailors who, upon detaching from the command, carry their competence throughout the Navy. Each of you, then, is both a product of the factory (when you learn) and a machine in the factory (when you help others learn).

What do you expect me to do?

I expect you to learn to be a better submariner each day. I challenge you to look at each field day, maintenance action, drill, monitor watch, underway, and deployment as an opportunity to learn more, and by doing so, to grow as a person.

Mechanism: We Learn (Everywhere, All the Time)

I began to look at our training program in a new light. It wasn't an administrative program, and it wasn't a program to minimize errors. Instead, it was a key enabler that allowed us to pass decision-making authority to lower and lower levels on *Santa Fe*.

Want to have a training program that employees will want to go to? Here's how it should work:

- The purpose of training is to increase technical competence.
- The result of increased technical competence is the ability to delegate increased decision making to the employees.
- Increased decision making among your employees will naturally result in greater engagement, motivation, and initiative.

You will end up with significantly higher productivity, morale, and effectiveness.

Divest Control, Increase Competence

Here's something to try at your next leadership meeting or corporate off-site.

1. Hand out a bunch of four-by-six cards and markers.
2. Start with this sentence completion: Our company would be more effective if [level] management could make decisions about [subject]. You specify the level of management but ask the group to fill in the subjects.
3. Once you have the set of cards, post them on the wall, and go on break. Let people mill around looking at what they've written.
4. Down-select to a couple subjects.
5. Ask this question: What, technically, do the people at this level of management need to know in order to make that decision?
6. Again, answer on the cards, post them, and go on break.

Now you'll have a relevant list of topics for training, and you can directly connect the training topics to increased employee decision making and control—in a word, empowerment.

When you set up the training, don't forget to communicate this thought process to the group. That way they'll know why they are going to attend training and want to attend, knowing it's their path to greater decision-making authority.

WE LEARN (EVERYWHERE, ALL THE TIME) is a mechanism for COMPETENCE.

I found "we learn" helped my internal mental balance and my perspective as well. In the past, I was both apprehensive and nervous prior to an inspection. I would be worried about how the ship would do and how our watch teams would perform. I would worry about the grades, the ship's reputation, and the potential embarrassment to me professionally. Perhaps the near-death of my career as a result of my experience on the *Will Rogers* is what made me edgy.

In any event, with the idea of learning in mind, I found myself in a state of calmness, even eagerness, as I thought about all that my crew and I would learn in the three days with a team of experts on board. My crew sensed this in me and reflected this attitude as well. Inspection teams would invariably comment on the eagerness of my crew to learn, and I had no doubt their earnestness caused more than one borderline grade to go our way.

QUESTIONS TO CONSIDER

- Are you aware of which areas in your business are marred by mistakes because the lower-level employees don't have enough technical competence to make good decisions?

- How could you implement a "we learn" policy among your junior and senior staff?
- Would you consider writing a creed for your organization modeled after the one we wrote for *Santa Fe*?
- Are people eager to go to training?

Under Way for San Diego

How do you get people to think "at the next level"? We discovered we had to change a fundamental practice that was inhibiting this.

February 22, 1999: Pearl Harbor, Hawaii (127 days to deployment)

"Captain, I intend to get under way. All departments report readiness, the tug is made up, we have permission from port operations."

"Very well."

"Cast off all lines."

On the bridge, Lieutenant Dave Adams was coaching a junior officer who was conning the submarine for the first time. We'd completed the upkeep maintenance period and were preparing to travel to San Diego for several exercises with the USS *Constellation* Battle Group. I had been in command forty-five days. We were scheduled to deploy with that same carrier battle group in four months. The transit and at-sea exercises would provide a welcome opportunity to work on our operational and war-fighting skills. Time at sea was invaluable for building the crew into a team. *Santa Fe*'s crew would be able to finish crafting our guiding principles, which had been delayed because I wanted the crew to develop them on their own. Now we would have the chance.

The transit out of Pearl Harbor was beautiful. I hardly said a word. Dave was coaching the young officer, and between the navigation team and the bridge party, I was getting a near-continuous stream of reports, status, intentions, and plans—all of it thinking out loud.

"Standby to mark the turn, next course is left to 182."

"Turning in approximately thirty seconds."

"Mark the turn by radar."

"That looks early to me."

"Mark the turn by visual."

"Helm, left fifteen degrees rudder, steady course 182."

"My rudder is left fifteen."

"The rudder is left."

"Turn looked a little late."

"Helm, increase your rudder to left twenty, steady 182."

Beautiful. The team was communicating well, in a mutually trusting and nonjudgmental way.

Pearl Harbor is a wonderful place to operate a submarine. Not only is it full of submarine lore and legend and beautiful weather; there is also deep water immediately offshore. On the East Coast, submarines must transit on the surface for miles to clear the continental shelf.

Santa Fe was assigned the water all around the harbor, and we were quickly at the dive point. I went below. Shortly afterward, the officer of the deck (OOD), lookouts, and conning officer came below after rigging the bridge for dive.

In the control room, men were taking their stations to submerge the ship. It was taking an irritatingly long time. Nuclear-powered subs spend so much time submerged that they rarely practice submerging. We'd lost focus on getting submerged and actually being a submarine. During World War II, when submarines spent most of their time on the surface, the crash dive was a matter of life and death. The men could clear the bridge, shut the hatch, and submerge in thirty seconds. Submerging on a nuclear-powered submarine was a much more graceful affair, taking several minutes. This wasn't the problem so much as the preparations for submerging. Again, here was evidence that a key war-fighting skill had atrophied.

Later, when we got under way, we would set an objective of minimizing the time from casting off lines to having *Santa Fe* submerged and stable at 150 feet underwater. That forced the crew not to think in terms of disparate events (under way, maneuvering watch, shift the watch below, submerge, trim the ship), with all the discontinuities in personnel and equipment, but to think of sticking all those events together. When challenged like that, they found ingenious ways to trim seconds and minutes from the transitions, which made *Santa Fe* a much more effective warship.

The diving officer of the watch (DOOW) announced that he would brief the dive. We were always briefing things. We love briefings in the military.

He opened the Ship System Manual (SSM), which contained the procedure, and began to read. "On the second blast of the diving alarm the Chief of the Watch will open all vents.

"The helmsman will place the rudder amidships."

On and on he droned.

Five minutes later, he asked if there were any questions.

There were none.

The first dive after an extended in-port raised my anxiety level for two reasons. First, the uncertainty in the trim of the ship is greater. If we brought on weight—whether additional torpedoes, equipment, stores, water, or even the number of crew—that wasn't properly accounted for, the submarine would be heavy, and sink. If we were lighter than expected, we'd open the vents and wallow on the surface for some time until we brought on enough water to achieve neutral buoyancy.

The other reason was that during the in-port period, while everyone was focused on maintenance, the crew would forget some of the nuances of the diving and submerging procedure. Like everyone else, we thought we were covering this by briefing the procedure.

And, because we needed to take every opportunity to learn, I intended to run some unexpected casualty drills, including simulating that certain gauges had malfunctioned.

"Captain, I intend to submerge the ship."

"Very well."

"Dive, submerge the ship."

"Submerge the ship. Dive, aye."

Well, needless to say, it didn't go well. Given unexpected indications, the team got confused. People took wrong actions initially and took too long to determine and correct the source of the problems.

Afterward, we gathered for a debrief, during which I simply asked, "What happened? The chief briefed the procedure." My flashlight was pointing at one of the planesmen, who hadn't responded properly when we simulated a stuck depth gauge.

"Captain, no one listens to those briefings."

"What do you mean?"

"Well, you come on watch, sit in the chair, and when the chief starts reading from the book, you're thinking, 'I already know how to do this,' so you don't listen too hard."

Mechanism: Don't Brief, Certify

That described a phenomenon I'd seen many times. A briefing is a passive activity for everyone except the briefer. Everyone else "is briefed." There is no responsibility for preparation or study. It's easy to just nod and say "ready" without full intellectual engagement. Furthermore, the sole responsibility in participating in a brief is to show up. Finally, a brief, as such, is not a decision point. The operation is going to happen and we are simply talking about it first.

We decided to do away with briefs. From that point on we would do certifications.

A certification is different from a brief in that during a certification, the person in charge of his team asks them questions. This could be the Chief in Charge—as in the case I'm recounting—or a lead surgeon prior to an operation. At the end of the certification, a decision is made whether or not the team is ready to perform the upcoming operation. If the team has not adequately demonstrated the necessary knowledge during the certification, the operation should be postponed.

The first time we tried it, the watch standers didn't know what they were supposed to do. They hadn't studied. When I asked them why they were unprepared, they told me they didn't know that we were going to submerge on this watch. Later, when I asked the same question of twenty watch standers for a major evolution like starting up the reactor, the excuse one sailor gave was that he knew we were going to start the reactor but didn't know what watch station he was going to be assigned to until immediately prior to the evolution.

What I learned from these examples is that briefing an action many times compensates for poor planning and that certification, which flows from the leader-leader approach, puts more work on management than leader-follower does because management needs not only to identify what near-term events will be accomplished but also the role each member of the team will be fulfilling.

Certifications shift the onus of preparation onto the participants. All participants are active. The change from passive briefs to active certification changed the crew's behavior. We found that when people know they will be asked questions they study their responsibilities ahead of time. This increases the intellectual involvement of the crew significantly. People are thinking about what they will be required to do and independently study for it.

Stop Briefing and Start Certifying in Your Business

Whenever you have focused team events, whether they are surgical procedures or sales pitches, think about the preparation.

Are people coming to "be briefed" or are they ready to present their portion of the event? In organizations where there are a lot of briefings, it will take extra work initially to shift the mind-set, but you could start with something as simple as read-ahead or think-ahead assignments that people are accountable for accomplishing.

The second thing that would make a big difference is to simply make sure the team knows that it's a decision meeting about whether they are ready to accomplish the procedure. Yes, the costs of saying "we're not ready" are high, but not as high as the costs of a bungled operation.

DON'T BRIEF, CERTIFY is a mechanism for COMPETENCE.

Certification is also a decision point. It is possible to fail a certification. Individuals can reveal that they aren't prepared to take part in an action because of their lack of knowledge or understanding. Otherwise, it's just a brief.

"Don't brief, certify" became another example where we basically did the opposite of what we were supposed to. Later on, we had fun when inspectors came to the ship and said they wanted to observe the brief prior to an evolution (like submerging) and I'd tell them we didn't do any briefings. A briefing was not required. What *was* required was that we operate the submarine safely and according to the procedures. And our certifications did this better than any briefing.

Don't brief, certify also became quite powerful because instead of one person studying an evolution and briefing it to the watch team, every crew member became responsible for knowing his job. It was a mechanism that forced intellectual engagement at every level in the crew. When you walked around the boat, you'd see guys studying. *Studying!* On their own! But only if management did their part. Some people call this ownership. A current management term is *employee engagement*.

An effective survey question to ask your employees is how many minutes a week they spend learning on their own, not mandated, not directed. Typically it's a small number. An organizational measure of improving health would be to increase that number. If you want engaged teams, don't brief, certify!

QUESTIONS TO CONSIDER

- How do you shift responsibility for performance from the briefer to the participants?
- How much preparation do people do prior to an event or operation?
- When was the last time you had a briefing on a project? Did listeners tune out the procedures?
- What would it take to start certifying that your project teams know what the goals are and how they are to contribute to them?
- Are you ready to assume more responsibility within the leader-leader model to identify what near-term events will be accomplished and the role each team member will fulfill?

All Present and Accounted For

ave you ever thought that people understood what you were talking about only to find out they didn't "get it" at all? Unfortunately, it happened on board *Santa Fe* and almost cost us a good sailor.

March 5, 1999: San Diego, California (116 days to deployment)

We'd arrived in San Diego an hour earlier and I was stewing over a report that showed multiple mechanical problems with our missile tubes. This was our first long underway where we started caring about their condition. Not surprisingly, when a system that is subjected to salt water and sea pressure is neglected, switches, connectors, and pressure sensors fail.

The COB appeared at my door. I was hoping to discuss our plan for getting this system 100 percent ready before the upcoming strike exercise.

"Sir, he said 'Fuck this shit' and left the boat."

"Huh, who?"

"Oh, I thought you knew. Sled Dog went AWOL."

Of course I knew him well. He was one of the junior quartermasters who had surprised me with their participation in improving our chart process.

Standing quartermaster of the watch (QMOW) is tough business. It's important for the safe navigation of the ship, and there is little room for error. Worse, it's under constant scrutiny because the watch is stood in the control room. While the OOD directly supervises the quartermaster, the XO and I frequently came into the control room and headed straight for the chart to see where we were. Frequently, the quartermaster would be attempting to plot his rounds with three or four officers crowding around the chart table. It is one of a handful of watch stations personally qualified by the captain.

My initial reaction was that I just didn't need this, and I slumped down in my chair.

I was already feeling bad. I had just realized that we were giving the Navy-wide advancement examinations this week. I had been preoccupied with the navigation of the submarine to San Diego and effective operations with the battle group and hadn't paid attention to the scheduling of the advancement exams. The Navy picks the dates and everyone takes the exams on the same day to prevent compromise. Performance on these exams would largely determine whether the one hundred petty officers on *Santa Fe* would be promoted. But because we hadn't been talking about the advancement exams and we hadn't scheduled any study time, I didn't have high hopes we had set the crew up for success.

Going AWOL (absent without leave) would be a permanent mark on Sled Dog's record, further hindering his potential to get promoted. It was also a serious indictment of how things were going on board *Santa Fe*.

After our problem with shore power and in the torpedo room, things started going better. A junior officer withdrew his resignation, and we started seeing reenlistment requests from the enlisted men. This was a sign that morale was turning around. Sled Dog's jumping ship would be a big setback.

We convened a meeting, a critique of sorts. Present were Sled Dog's chain of command, including Lieutenant Commander Bill Greene and Chief John Larson, as well as the COB, the XO, and me. There were two camps. On one side, several of the senior enlisted men and chiefs pointed out that Sled Dog had been in the Navy for several years, was perfectly sober, knew what he was doing, and knew what the consequences of his actions were. He was on his own, and they already had a report chit written up on him that would send him to captain's mast. It would be important for good order and discipline to deal with him harshly, especially with deployment looming. We didn't want sailors thinking they could renege on their obligation to the nation and their shipmates.

On the other side, the officers were more sympathetic. They pointed out that the quartermasters had been standing port and starboard watch since we left Pearl Harbor a week ago. That meant Sled Dog had stood watch six hours on, six hours off. Of course, you have to eat, prepare for watch, and conduct postwatch duties during those "six hours off," so it ends up being more like eight hours on, four hours off. Then there are training sessions, briefs, and all-hands drills. If they occurred during your sleep time, too bad. In this case, we had had piloting certifications, run drills, and shifted the clocks two hours ahead to match the local San Diego time. All of these factors had, unfortunately, conspired to reduce Sled Dog's sleep in the previous thirty-six hours to zero. No one planned it, but no one was looking out for him either. We then had several hours piloting the ship into San Diego. This is a period of intense activity while we bring the ship into port, especially for the quartermasters.

While Sled Dog wasn't going to win awards as the top-ranking petty officer in his division, he was a hard worker and a valuable member of the watch team. If we lost him, *Santa Fe* would be unable to get under way. If we were already port and starboard then we'd be down to "port and re-port," which meant we had only one qualified watch stander for the quartermaster watch station. This would be a severe limitation to the ship's ability to act in the nation's defense.

The Tip of the Iceberg?

I decided to dig deeper into the problem.

Q: Why were the quartermasters port and starboard anyway?
    A: Because there weren't enough of them to support the normal three-section watch bill.

Q: Why not?
    A: The chief of that division hadn't gotten enough of his guys qualified; we had a perilously shallow bench. The qualification program was broken.

Q: Was anyone else qualified who could have made them three-section instead of port and starboard?
    A: Yes, the leading first class petty officer of that division (a supervisor), but he was "off the watch bill" in order to be ready to stand the discretionary watch "navigation supervisor" (NavSupe).

Q: But isn't the navigation supervisor stationed to increase safety of the navigation picture when the ship is close to land?
    A: Yes.

Q: And didn't we just cross the eastern Pacific Ocean, from Hawaii to San Diego?
    A: Yes.

Q: And did we need a navigation supervisor?
    A: No.

This pissed me off. This supervisor was letting his guys go without sleep and he wasn't even on the watch bill.

I reviewed the entire watch bill more carefully and realized that the diving officer of the watch—a watch stood by the chiefs—was one in six. In other words, they shared one watch station among six qualified chiefs, one six-hour watch every thirty-six hours. Meantime, the standard crew rotation was one in three—three men per watch station, and some watch stations, like Sled Dog's, was one in two—two men for the one watch station.

How did that happen? It was the normal way of doing business on submarines. Some boats take their chiefs entirely off the watch bill. That this could be viewed as an acceptable way of doing business was a manifestation of the idea that being a chief meant you had more privileges, not more responsibility. It was the "good life" that the junior enlisted were supposed to aspire to. But it had the opposite effect: all it did was alienate the crew. I was upset that the chiefs had taken care of themselves first, and the crew was paying for it.

"Where is Sled Dog now?" I asked.

No one was sure, but he was seen heading toward the barracks, the on-base housing for the crew. I thought about that. Why would someone go to the on-base barracks if they wanted to go AWOL? And thinking about what Sled Dog had been through, I'm pretty sure I would have said "Fuck this shit" as well.

By this point I was firmly in the sympathetic camp, but I was having trouble convincing the chiefs that we had an obligation to try and find him. I could have ordered it, but that would have resulted in forced compliance. I decided to find him myself. I departed the ship and headed over to the enlisted barracks a couple blocks from where we were moored at Submarine Base San Diego on Point Loma. I found the barracks manager and, amazingly, Sled Dog had registered and had a room. Strange behavior if he was quitting the Navy. I went to his room and knocked. He was there!

I needed to be careful because I didn't want to say anything that exonerated his behavior or manifested my displeasure with the chiefs. At the same time, I was sympathetic to his lack of sleep and the uneven treatment he'd received. I had the report chit written up on him in my hand. Going AWOL carries steep penalties. He could be restricted to the ship for sixty days, which would keep him on the ship for a major part of the in-port time prior to deployment; he could lose a month's pay; and he could get busted down a rank.

We had a conversation. I could see he was emotionally and physically exhausted. In a dramatic move, I tore up the report chit and granted him amnesty but made it clear he needed to be back on the ship the following morning. He probably didn't know it, but I had tainted any potential captain's mast I might hold on him by getting personally involved. If it ever went to a court-martial, a lawyer would have a field day. I was betting we would never need to go that far.

I went back to *Santa Fe* and mustered the chiefs. I reviewed what we'd been through and reminded them of the January meeting we'd had in the old periscope shop in Pearl Harbor. I was upset because it seemed like in some cases they'd taken the increased authority I'd given them and used that to make their own situations easier. Some were missing the sense of obligation toward their men. "Weren't we all in a meeting together back in January when you accepted responsibility for your men and for running the ship? Didn't we all understand that that meant being involved, participating, sharing the pain with the crew, not acting like some privileged aristocracy?" I was barking out these words and gesturing toward them with the flashlight. I was pissed.

Well, yes.

I told the chiefs about the deal I made with Sled Dog. Some thought I was setting a bad precedent.

Had they been dishonest in January? I don't think so. I just don't think they could picture how much different it would be if they started walking the talk.

No wonder the crew was demoralized, with this kind of

behavior going on. No wonder *Santa Fe* had reenlisted merely three guys the entire previous year. I had an overwhelming urge to take all authority away from the chiefs, to take "local and immediate control" to get them on board. This, of course, would have been entirely expected and made me like every other leader.

The next morning the COB came in with his daily muster report.

"Captain, all present and accounted for."

He turned and departed. We both knew that meant Sled Dog had returned as promised.

Not all the chiefs were happy with the resolution of the Sled Dog issue. Some worried that I had set a bad standard and that there would be an erosion of military discipline. They feared a host of AWOLs, and if I held those sailors accountable, it would be hypocritical. It was suggested there would be an appearance of favoritism—maybe even a perception that I'd shown deference in the case of a minority. Turns out their predictions were wrong. We never had another AWOL in three years.

I resisted taking more control and continued to let the COB and XO manage the enlisted watch bill. After I got over my anger, I invoked the following rule of "watch bill equitability": no supervisory watch station could be in a watch rotation better than the worst rotation of any watch station reporting to that supervisor. As this would work its way up the chain, there would be no way the chiefs or officers would be better off than the crew. This wasn't taken well, but I needed to get the point across, and I was tired of trying to explain things in a noncoercive way. They would just have to experience it.

Mechanism: Continually and Consistently Repeat the Message

The issue I had the hardest time coming to grips with was how I didn't know all this was happening. Technically, the XO signs the enlisted watch bill so, technically, I wasn't responsible. Still, I was. I had been in the control room a hundred times during the previous week. I'd frequently seen Sled Dog standing there on watch. Sure, I had excuses. I was focused on other things, whereas managing the watch bill was the direct responsibility of others. No matter how I rationalized it, however, I felt responsible. Perhaps this sense of responsibility colored my actions and perhaps it could have come out badly. Had I carefully weighed the potential impact to me personally, I would never have gone in body to the enlisted barracks. I didn't think like that, though. I was only worried about my sailor, who was off by himself and dealing with senior management that wasn't trying to get him on board.

Again, I resigned myself to the fact that my new approach to leadership wasn't working. It was too hard, and if the chiefs didn't get it, how could we be successful? I considered going back to barking orders and demanding rigid compliance. Upon reflection, that wasn't the leader I wanted to be, and I was convinced that my original course was right: giving people authority, paired with responsibility and the tools to do the job, would pay off in the end. I resisted this urge and decided we had to stay the course.

The behavior of the chiefs was totally baffling to me. After two months under my command, how could they not get what we were trying to do? I'd given them much greater authority with Chiefs in Charge; they'd helped write the guiding principles; they'd heard me talk a hundred times about how we were going to run things on *Santa Fe*. It seemed as if there were some evil force that was pushing against us and kept people in the same old way of thinking.

What I realized, however, is the need for a relentless, consistent repetition of the message.

CONTINUALLY AND CONSISTENTLY REPEAT THE MESSAGE is a mechanism for COMPETENCE.

Repeat the same message day after day, meeting after meeting, event after event. Sounds redundant, repetitive, and boring. But what's the alternative? Changing the message? That results in confusion and a lack of direction. I didn't realize the degree to which old habits die hard, even when people are emotionally on board with the change. The chiefs wanted to be on board, but they pictured a leadership approach, a style, they'd seen before on the "USS *Ustafish*"—the generic term for the submarine I "used to" be on. They just pictured something from their past. It was hard for them to create an image of what we were trying to accomplish. It was something brand new. There wasn't an existing example or movie we could point to.

When you bring in something new, something that has never been seen before, you can talk about it and some will get it. On *Santa Fe*, we did have some chiefs who got it immediately. Senior Chief Worshek got it. Chief Larson got it. Some would get it soon; others would take longer. I discovered that what happens when you explain a change is that the crew hears what you say, but they are thinking, "Oh yeah, I know what he's talking about. That's like it was on the USS *Ustafish*." They hear and think they know what you mean, but they don't. They've never had a picture of what you are talking about. They can't see in their imagination how it works. They are not being intentionally deceitful; they just are not picturing what you are picturing.

Moreover, if they understand what you mean they might be skeptical that this new way of doing business, which is different from anything they've seen before, could be better. How is it possible to be in the Navy for (fill in the years) and not have seen this?

In order to help me remember this and keep my cool, I had a poster made. I got the idea from an article titled "It's a Dog's Life," which I'd read in the November 1995 issue of *Fast Company*. It profiled VeriFone's then-CEO Hatim Tyabji. In the poster, I am standing in front of my dog Barclay saying "Sit." The dog was standing. The first eight frames were identical. "Sit, sit, sit," etc. No recriminations, no admonishments, just "sit." In the ninth and last frame, Barclay is sitting and the caption is "Good dog." I hung this on the back of my stateroom door. Since my door was open most of the time, visitors didn't see it, but I would.

- Are any of your employees on the brink of going AWOL because they're overworked and underappreciated?
- When is it right for the leader to overturn protocol in the effort to rescue a single stressed-out subordinate?
- What messages do you need to keep repeating in your business to make sure your management team doesn't take care of themselves first, to the neglect of their teams?

Final Preparations

Do you believe that allowing initiative from the bottom won't work in a crisis? I learned that even in casualties (emergencies), releasing control yields better results.

May 1999: Under Way from Pearl Harbor to San Diego (28 days to deployment)

At sea again, *Santa Fe* was heading back to San Diego. We needed this time to run a complete set of drills and hone our operational skills. Our final certification for deployment (POMCERT) would happen once we got to San Diego. While it was coming faster than I would have liked, there was a lot going right on *Santa Fe*. Our sailors were submitting reenlistment requests, and maintenance was going well for the first time. Watch officers were solving problems and department heads were talking to each other. Deliberate action was reducing errors, and more and more of the crew were becoming believers. The chiefs continued to grow into their Chiefs in Charge authority. What started with managing leave chits had now grown into controlling schedules and managing qualifications. We had gotten through the backlog of crew members awaiting tests and interviews for qualification, and the average time to qualify in submarines was steadily marching down. Now when I arrived on board in the morning, the ship was already a beehive of activity as opposed to a bunch of guys waiting for permission.

Still, I wasn't certain that we would be ready for deployment. The past six weeks had been ones of frenetic activity and tension. After returning to Pearl Harbor, the submarine went into a maintenance period, our last opportunity for nine months to do major maintenance. I had a long list of equipment worries, including sonar equipment, the oxygen generator, missile and torpedo tubes, and updates to the electronics and software for the combat control system, to name a few. Additionally, although we would perform many daily, weekly, and monthly maintenance routines while on deployment to keep our equipment in peak condition, the less frequent routine maintenance would need to be done now. Somehow the crew had gotten it all done and we had gotten under way. We always had the goal of performing training during these maintenance periods, but it rarely happened. Now we had a week to make it all up. There was no going back on our management experiment now—we were going to sink or swim with our new approach.

"Fire, Fire, Fire!"

A fire on a submarine was one of the most life-threatening accidents we could have. Not only would thick black smoke force us to wear our emergency air breathing (EAB) devices; the visibility would be reduced to near zero. Unchecked, the fire would grow in size, and the contained atmosphere in the boat would result in heat and pressure increases that would make human existence impossible. Eleven years previously, in April 1988, a fire aboard the USS *Bonefish* killed three sailors. In that fire, the heat got so intense that the shoes of crew members standing on the deck above the fire melted.

The key time was two minutes. Studies showed we needed a fire hose applying water to the fire within two minutes.

I was standing just forward of the crew's mess, which was full of nukes in training, when the fire alarm rang. The department heads ran the drill programs but I approved all the drills, including when and how they would start. The engineer had briefed the drill monitors that the fire would be in the storeroom just aft of the crew's mess. I wanted to see what would happen because I had been previously frustrated that it took too long to get immediate extinguishing agents and fire hoses to the fire.

The closest fire hose on *Santa Fe* was in the passageway just forward of the crew's mess, about fifty feet from the fire's location.

It should have been easy. The entire engineering department, forty people, was conducting training in the crew's mess.

The fire was detected and the alarm was sounded. What happened next?

Well, the nukes scattered, running right by the hose and leaving it hanging on the bulkhead. The crew members assigned to that particular hose couldn't even get to the hose because there were so many nukes in the way. Why didn't the nukes just take the hose, lay it out, pressurize it, and end the whole thing in sixty seconds?

Because the submarine force hadn't trained them to do that. Following standard procedure that the Navy had encouraged as a "best practice," we had determined that watch standers on duty would man the hoses. This was originally decided because in the event of a fire at 0300, we couldn't count on enough crew members to be up and about to self-organize into an effective response. So we identified watch standers as contingency firefighters who would leave their watch stations and deal with the fire. This was an exception to normal practice; leaving your watch station unattended was not allowed.

Over the next few years, as ships were evaluated by various inspection teams, the inspectors would stand there with a clipboard and ask the nozzleman, when he showed up, who he was. "I'm the on-watch auxiliaryman forward." The inspector would look at the watch bill and make sure he was the one identified. If not, it would be a deficiency, a watch bill violation.

This was another example of where the procedure had become the master and not the servant. The motivation had shifted from putting the fire out to following the procedure. As a result, we got the crazy behavior observed on the mess deck of *Santa Fe*.

Yet another problem was underlying and distorting the crew's behavior. There was no incentive for the crew to put the simulated fire out early.

Drill guides at the time foretold a prescriptive set of events. They weren't connected in any way to the crew's response. For instance, even if the crew immediately brought a portable extinguisher the fire would grow. Even if the crew arrived with a pressurized fire hose in less than two minutes and applied water to the base of the fire—using appropriate firefighting techniques, wearing the right equipment and hard-soled shoes—the fire would spread more. It would require multiple hoses and a sustained attack to douse the fire. The submarine would fill with smoke and we would need to go to periscope depth and ventilate. It was a one-hour drill. The thinking behind the guides was that the crew needed to be drilled on and prepared for all possible outcomes.

We changed all that.

Mechanism: Specify Goals, Not Methods

First, we attacked the motivation problem. We authorized the drill monitor at the scene to adapt the drill based on the crew's response.

If the crew applied a portable extinguisher in the first forty-five seconds, the fire was out. *Done.*

If it took two minutes to get a pressurized hose to the scene, the fire was out. *Done.*

These consequences modeled nature.

Now the crew was motivated to actually do what we wanted them to do: attack the fire with portable fire extinguishers and pressurized fire hoses, unencumbered by administrative disincentives and distractions.

Next, I explained to the crew that our objective was to put the fire out, and I didn't care who was on the hose. They responded, and we significantly improved our response time. Now when the alarm sounded, the closest men self-organized to achieve the goal. We would later receive awards for our damage control responses.

We also revamped another aspect of responding to casualties like fires.

The force-wide practice was to use terse commands when responding to casualties. For example, during a fire, the man at the scene must verbally paint a picture of what he is seeing. We didn't have a set of video cameras monitoring the spaces; as a result, the CO in control or others around the ship would not know how extensive the fire was. And our limited language got in the way: all we had was the word *fire* to cover the spectrum from a wall of flames to a smoking dryer lint trap. Our practice was to use the standard word, but then we started adding context, such as whether there were "open flames" or not. This mechanism of describing what you see is an extension of thinking out loud.

The officers who manned damage control central, or DC central, controlled the ship's response to casualties. DC central consisted of a department head set up in my stateroom with charts and status boards and phone talkers.

We started to explain to the crew that the casualty drill going forward would be different. We figured, why not just tell them what needed to happen? After all, in the case of a real casualty, this is exactly what I'd want them to do. So, in clear, concise sentences, we'd tell them, "Crew members in the vicinity should attack the fire with portable extinguishers." And DC central would announce things like "A thermal imager is needed in the auxiliary room." DC central would not specify who or how. The crew figured it out. The man with the thermal imager would head to the auxiliary room and, as he passed a phone talker, report, "Senior Chief Worshek with the thermal imager proceeding to the auxiliary room." Again, this was "thinking out loud."

We found this "decentralized" approach to DC central to be much more effective.

We turned other practices on their head as well, such as the important practice of keeping the ship quiet. Stealth is life for a submarine, and minimizing unnecessary bangs and noises is the lifeblood of every submarine.

I was standing in the control room one evening and my sonar chief, Senior Chief Worshek, announced from the sonar room, "Loud transient, own ship." A transient was a temporary noise from within *Santa Fe*. It could be caused by any number of things, from carelessly dropping a wrench on the deck plates in the engine room to opening an air valve too quickly. This wasn't uncommon; sonar would continuously monitor *Santa Fe* and announce these sound violations.

At this point, the standard practice would be for the chief of the watch (COW) to call every watch stander on the ship and find out what they were all doing so that we could determine the source of the transient. It was top-down management.

But this time Senior Chief Worshek walked into the control room and suggested we change the practice. Instead of us (in the control room) hunting down the violation, we told the watch standers that if they made a transient they should just call the COW and report it without being prompted. This would save a lot of time, and it turned the handling of this issue of the stealth of the submarine from a top-down approach (*We will force you to be stealthy, by God*) to one where everyone felt an obligation to maintain the stealth of the ship.

We tried it.

Not everyone was sure this would work. First of all it was different. Old-timers grumbled that we'd lose our acoustic superiority if we let the crew make whatever noise they wanted to so long as they just confessed.

Once again, however, it didn't turn out that way. We started getting many more reports of transients than those detected by sonar. No one yelled; no one criticized. We just analyzed when, why, and how the noisy events occurred. They were things like pressurizing tanks, shifting valves under pressure, using hydraulics, or shifting steam or lube oil system lineups. Many occurred back in the engine room, and because the main sonar was in the bow they would go undetected.

By unemotionally addressing all the transients that occurred rather than only the ones that our monitoring system detected, we ended up with a quieter ship.

We arrived in San Diego to pick up the inspectors. The night before the inspection, I found that I was quite serene internally about this major test of my leadership ability and the crew. Normally, the vulnerability of being responsible for the performance of the ship yet delegating almost all of the control would have left me anxious. I attributed my peace to my attitude of learning and curiosity.

My confidence was justified. The crew performed superbly and Commodore Mark Kenny certified us for deployment. I was happy to see a large portion of the crew using the three-name rule. Our reputation was riding high. All we needed to do now was return to Pearl Harbor, execute a couple weeks of final preparations and load-outs, and we'd be under way for deployment on June 18, ready to go two weeks early.

Specifying to the crew that the true objective was to put the fire out as quickly as possible was a mechanism primarily for competence. SPECIFYING GOALS, NOT METHODS is a mechanism for COMPETENCE. In our case, this was because the crew was motivated to devise the best approach to putting out the fire. Once they were freed from following a prescribed way of doing things they came up with many ingenious ways to shave seconds off our response time. As another example, we had always berthed the crew strictly according to rank. They realized that certain damage control equipment was easier to get to from some bunks than others. By rearranging the berthing plan and assigning those bunks to the men who had responsibility for the nearby damage control equipment, they were able to respond faster. In a way, SPECIFYING GOALS also served as a mechanism for CLARITY by focusing on achieving excellence rather than avoiding errors. We found over and over again on *Santa Fe* that compliance with the procedures had supplanted accomplishing the objective as the ultimate goal. Although we don't want people to founder, and we want adherence to procedures and best practices, we nevertheless should be on guard against this tendency.

The problem with specifying the method along with the goal is one of diminished control.

Provide your people with the objective and let them figure out the method.

QUESTIONS TO CONSIDER

- Have your processes become the master rather than the servant?

- How can you ensure adherence to procedure while at the same time ensuring that accomplishing the objective remains foremost in everyone's mind?
- Have you reviewed your operations manual lately to replace general terminology with clear, concise, specific directions?
- Are your staff complying with procedures to the neglect of accomplishing the company's overall objectives?

PART IV

CLARITY

As more decision-making authority is pushed down the chain of command, it becomes increasingly important that everyone throughout the organization understands what the organization is about. This is called clarity, and it is the second supporting leg—along with competence—that is needed in order to distribute control.

Clarity means people at all levels of an organization clearly and completely understand what the organization is about. This is needed because people in the organization make decisions against a set of criteria that includes what the organization is trying to accomplish. If clarity of purpose is misunderstood, then the criteria by which a decision is made will be skewed, and suboptimal decisions will be made.

The chapters in this part will introduce you to the mechanisms we devised to implement leader-leader practices by stressing clarity. The mechanisms described are these:

- Achieve excellence, don't just avoid errors (this was introduced in chapter 7).

- Build trust and take care of your people.
- Use your legacy for inspiration.
- Use guiding principles for decision criteria.
- Use immediate recognition to reinforce desired behaviors.
- Begin with the end in mind.
- Encourage a questioning attitude over blind obedience.

Under Way for Deployment

How can you take care of your people? Turns out, there are lots of ways.

June 18, 1999: Pearl Harbor, Hawaii (deployed!)

We'd done it. I'd been in command of *Santa Fe* for 161 days and we were ready to deploy, two weeks early. Everything was ready for our deployment: stores loaded, weapons loaded and checked, all personnel on board, reactor operating and main engines warmed up. The tug was tied up alongside, ready to pull *Santa Fe* away from the pier and back us into the channel. At that point, we would cast off from the tug and head out the main shipping channel toward the Pacific Ocean. No inspectors, no riders, no straphangers. Just 135 highly empowered sailors eager to serve their country.

Santa Fe would head west from Pearl Harbor and make a stop in Japan. For several weeks thereafter, we would operate in the western Pacific before transiting the Strait of Malacca between Singapore and Indonesia into the Indian Ocean and then across to the Middle East. We'd then operate in and around the Arabian Sea for a couple of months before returning to Pearl Harbor. Altogether, we would be gone for six months.

On the pier, a large group of wives and children and other family members stood together. As we cast off the lines and tossed them to the pier, we sounded one prolonged blast from the whistle. Most of the family members looked up at the bridge.

In that moment, I realized exactly what my job was. I was to take these 134 men under my command thousands of miles from home, potentially engaging in combat, and bring them back safely to all those upturned faces. It gave me a renewed sense of purpose.

The transit out the channel went quickly, and we were soon submerged and heading west. I gathered the chiefs and officers and we discussed what we wanted to accomplish. "Look, we're going to be gone for six months," Lieutenant Commander Rick Panlilio advocated. "We should encourage each person in the crew to establish personal goals—take courses, read books, exercise, that kind of thing—in addition to the goals we have for *Santa Fe.*"

I agreed and was impressed that after everything we'd done to get ready for deployment, he didn't just want to take a long nap.

Rick was right. I asked around to get a pulse of the crew on this idea. Chief David Steele was enthusiastic. He wanted to start taking courses toward a college degree. The Navy has a program for that, but most people don't have the time or the initiative to take advantage of it.

We decided to let the chiefs talk to their sailors about their individual goals, but we'd define some ship-wide goals for everyone to focus on during the deployment. We came up with three themes: empowerment, efficiency, and tactical excellence. When we were done, we discussed whether or not we should tell people off the ship about our intentions. I thought, why not? It seemed to me that writing down our three ship-wide goals in an outgoing message would add clarity to our thinking, keep my bosses informed about what we were doing, and add weight to our initiatives.

Here's the message we transmitted to our superiors on June 21, a little before crossing the international date line. I deliberately sent it to as broad an audience as possible.

From: USS *Santa Fe*
Subject: *Santa Fe* deployment objectives

Remarks:

1. *Santa Fe* express is now headed west. My officers and crew are looking forward to the challenges and opportunities of being deployed on the front lines for our nation's security. . . .

2. Working with my department heads and senior advisers . . . I have set empowerment efficiency and tactical excellence as the guiding themes for continuously improving our performance during deployment.

>   a. Empowerment: I intend to empower the crew to achieve their personal and professional goals through initiatives such as a focused effort to improve advancement exam performance, encouraging PACE [Program for Afloat College Education] and other independent study programs, and providing incentives for increased physical conditioning. I further intend to push authority and responsibility downward wherever practical to improve job satisfaction. This is a continuation of a theme I have already started to work on and I think we are having some success. I already have ten crewmen who have submitted reenlistment requests for the gulf. [Reenlisting in the Arabian Gulf carried tax benefits.]
>
>   b. Efficiency: reaching our empowerment goals will require us to significantly improve crew efficiency . . .

we will strive for greater efficiency in everything from running tighter drill scenarios to removing inefficiencies in meal preparation and service.

c. Tactical excellence: I intend to continue our pursuit of tactical excellence by encouraging innovative methods of leveraging Santa Fe's combat power with particular emphasis on submarine support to the battle group, national tasking, strike warfare and special operations. . . .

3. I am working to establish measures of effectiveness for each of our goals. I will keep you posted on our progress toward empowerment, efficiency, and tactical excellence.

Very respectfully, CDR David Marquet.

Mechanism: Build Trust and Take Care of Your People

During the first few days out of port, I spent a fair amount of time walking about the ship. We'd received some bad news: the promotion announcements were in, based on the advancement examinations, and we hadn't done well. I knew this was tough on the men after all the work they had done getting Santa Fe ready for deployment and after leaving their families for six months. I wanted to get a sense of just how much that disappointment was affecting the crew.

The more I saw and heard, the more I became aware that we'd done a great disservice to our crew back in March regarding the advancement exams. I vowed to do something about it, but one thing that continued to trouble me was why I had to drive this from the top. Couldn't we get the chiefs themselves involved in their own guys' advancement prospects? After all, as chiefs they had somehow figured out how to get advanced, that's why they were chiefs. I kept this gripe to myself and focused on understanding the problem.

The first issue was that our crew—by which I mean the enlisted men who were not yet chiefs, and made up 80 percent of the ship's company—did not thoroughly understand how the advancement system worked. The crew had heard so many myths and had been given so much misinformation, they had come to believe that the advancement system was a mystical process over which they had no control. It was this issue of control that we had to attack first.

The process worked like this: All petty officers received a composite advancement score after taking the exam to determine if they would be advanced. This composite score was made up of a weighing of the following marks: a score for their performance evaluation marks; a score for their grade on the Navy-wide advancement examination; and scores for awards, time in the Navy, time in rate, and the number of times they'd previously taken the exam but not been advanced. Roughly a third of the final composite was based on the performance evaluation marks, a third was based on the examination, and a third was based on the remaining components.

Not everyone who is eligible gets promoted. The higher positions are scarce. There are several reasons why promotions are not unlimited. First, the number of jobs gets smaller as the ranks get higher. This pyramid is a deliberate personnel-planning mechanism for the Navy. Even if the Navy wanted to promote everyone eligible, they can't because Congress appropriates money for the Navy's personnel programs and pay, and hence sets a cap on how many people the Navy can have at each rank level. The naval personnel command would then determine the cutoff score based on how many total openings we had for the next higher rank. Sailors below that level were "PNA" (Passed, Not Advanced). This meant that they'd passed the exam but did not achieve a final multiple high enough for advancement.

Fortunately, the Navy provides each command with detailed results for each person who took the test. In the past, we'd always handed these sheets to the sailors and let them deal with it on an individual basis. This time, I made a copy of all of the results and

performed some mathematical analysis on the aggregate popula-
tion. I had spreadsheets of the data. I spent hours sorting, cor-
relating, and graphing the data.

The analysis showed that even though the exam made up
about 33 percent of the total score it accounted for more than 80
percent of the variation in points between those who were
advanced and those who were not. In all the other components
that made up the final multiple—performance marks as well as
awards, time in Navy, and time in rate, et cetera—the candidates
were tightly grouped and the difference between those advanced
and those not advanced was small. The exam, therefore, made all
the difference. Our guys had averaged fifty-one points on the
exam, whereas the average sailor who was advanced averaged
sixty-four. Guys who were losing ten to twenty points on the exam
couldn't make it up with a couple of extra awards. You'd need ten
Navy Achievement Medals to do that.

Ironically, this was great news, because examination performance was something we could control. My overwhelming theme
for the men would be "You CAN get advanced, and we CAN help
you." We went to work fixing this.

Next, we looked at the areas in which our petty officers did
poorly. Again, the detailed reports the Navy provided had the
detailed data, but they needed to be analyzed in an aggregated
manner. The yeomen did poorly on "travel administration." Well,
arranging travel wasn't something you did as a yeoman assigned
to a submarine, so we augmented that topic with training. The
auxiliarymen did poorly on "fuels." On a conventional ship, the
management of fuels is a key activity, but not so much on a nuclear
submarine, so we needed additional training there. We decided
to give practice examinations. As the petty officers were studying
for the next exam cycle, we asked them to write down sample
multiple-choice questions based on what they were reading. In
addition to shifting their study habits from passive reading to
actively thinking about test questions, we began to generate our
own internal "advancement exam," sprinkling these multiple-

choice questions into our continuing training program. These did not entirely replace but rather augmented the short-answer questions we normally tested on. We also made our questions harder than the ones on the actual advancement examination. For example, our multiple-choice questions could have none, one, or more than one right answer. This required significantly more in-depth knowledge and helped build on the technical competence of the crew. Prior to the September advancement exam (the dates are Navy-wide, in March and September) we gave full practice advancement exams. Rather than looking at the advancement process as a separate activity, we integrated it into the operations of the submarine. Now all our interests were aligned.

Taking Care of Your People Extends Beyond Their Work Lives

Our first stop after transiting the western Pacific would be Okinawa, Japan. Okinawa is in the middle of the Ryuku island chain, which stretches in an arc from the southern tip of the main island group of Japan to Taiwan, six hundred miles away. Okinawa was the scene of a major battle in World War II between April and June 1945. Currently it is the home of a U.S. Marine Corps base. As we approached Okinawa, two things became apparent.

First, the XO who was on *Santa Fe* when I arrived would be transferring to spend time with his father, who was ill.

Lieutenant Commander Tom Stanley, his replacement, would have to be transferred aboard and would now be the XO for the deployment. This was an unusual personnel transfer because Tom was coming from a staff job in Pearl Harbor, had not attended the Prospective Executive Officer course, and hadn't spent any time doing the workup with the ship. I needed to justify this highly unusual move. The argument we made went like this: where would he learn more, on deployment on an operational submarine or back in the classroom in New London? The answer, of course, was on the submarine. The question we had neither asked nor answered, however, was how would the submarine cope with an XO who needed training from day one?

The second decision had to do with my engineer, Rick Panlilio. Rick's wife was pregnant and would likely have their baby in the next couple of weeks. I sorely wanted to transfer Rick off in Okinawa. It's hard enough to justify transferring the engineer at any time during deployment, but with the simultaneous transfer of the XO, I thought it was going to be a tough sell. Still, I had missed my daughter's birth in 1989 because my command (the *Will Rogers* again) wouldn't let me go in time. I wanted to fix past wrongs.

I gathered the leadership team and we discussed it. I wasn't sure how to convince our operational boss to approve the plan. All communication would have to go through standard Navy message traffic, no face-to-face, no video, no phone call. Like so many times, my not knowing the answer ahead of time helped me. Instead of a scripted meeting where I pretended to solicit ideas, we had an honest conversation. At the end, we thought that if we presented a well-thought-out plan to Rear Admiral Joseph Krol, who as Commander, Submarine Group Seven, in Japan, was our operational commander, it would be approved. Lieutenant Commander Bill Greene went off to draft the message we would send. In the end, it looked like this:

From: USS *Santa Fe*
To: SUBGRU Seven
Subj: Personnel transfer

---

1. Admiral, my engineer's wife is due to have their baby at any moment . . . although sending two of the ship's most senior officers (the xo and engineer) off just prior to . . . transit . . . would be imprudent for most ships, my

wardroom is so rife with talented jo's [junior officers] that it affords me the opportunity to do this. Lt. Brooks will be acting eng, and as I have stated, he is a superb naval officer . . . additionally, I have two top-notch navigation supervisors in addition to the nav. The eng is a dedicated professional and is not pushing for this; however, I know he would be disappointed not to be there and I feel I can safely put him on leave.

It worked! The plan was approved. This was possible only because the ship had demonstrated superior skills, and through our implementation of the leader-leader structure we had developed an extensive pool of talent. Here is where it all paid off—one officer was with his father at a critical time and another officer was there for his child's birth. (Rick got there in time.)

Our efforts to improve the petty officers' performance on the advancement exams were rewarded as well. Months later, the COB walked in with a smile. He handed me the advancement results. I scanned down the sheet and was happy to see that YN2 Scott Dillon was now YN1 Scott Dillon. His next step would be to compete for chief. We had done significantly better than the previous year. Overall in 1999, we advanced forty-eight enlisted men, 40 percent of the enlisted crew. By explaining the process to the crew and giving them the tools to improve their performance, we empowered them to determine their own success. We would do even better in 2000 and 2001.

There were not a lot of things I could do for the crew to get them more money other than ensuring that they had the best opportunity for advancement. I worked hard on that. Because the crew was convinced that I was "on their team" there were never any issues with negative responses to constructive criticism. It was never a "me versus you" issue. Had they not believed I was doing everything I could for them, it would have been a lot tougher when I asked them to work so hard.

BUILDING TRUST AND TAKING CARE OF YOUR PEOPLE is a mechanism for CLARITY.

I worked hard to overcome my natural intolerance of inadequacies and my blunt speaking, but I didn't always succeed. I found, over time, that when I blurted out criticism people didn't mind. They didn't take it personally because they knew that two weeks previously I had been doing everything possible to get them promoted.

It's hard to find a leadership book that doesn't encourage us to "take care of our people." What I learned is this: Taking care of your people does not mean protecting them from the consequences of their own behavior. That's the path to irresponsibility. What it does mean is giving them every available tool and advantage to achieve their aims in life, beyond the specifics of the job. In some cases that meant further education; in other cases crewmen's goals were incompatible with Navy life and they separated on good terms.

QUESTIONS TO CONSIDER

- What would you and your team like to accomplish?
- How can you as a leader help your people accomplish it?
- Are you doing everything you can to make tools available to your employees to achieve both professional and personal goals?
- Are you unintentionally protecting people from the consequences of their own behavior?

22

A Remembrance of War

D o you have a rich organizational legacy? We did, but we weren't using it.

July 2, 1999: Western Pacific Ocean (in command)

"580 feet, 23 down, 18 knots."

Santa Fe was pitching rapidly toward the ocean bottom. Just because we were certified and deployed didn't mean we stopped running casualty drills. This was a jam dive from high speed. It simulates a failure of the stern planes in the maximum downward position. At high speeds, it is a dangerous condition because the submarine rapidly pitches downward.

We had taken the appropriate immediate actions. All back emergency, full rise on the bow planes, emergency blowing the forward ballast tanks.

"600 feet, 25 down, 14 knots."

"6-1-0 feet, 2-6 down, 1-2 knots." Still going down but at a slower rate. The diving officer of the watch (DOOW) was calling out the depth, down angle, and speed so everyone in the control room would know it. He sat just behind the planesman and had the clearest sight of the panel indicating what was happening with ship control. He slowed down his voice as the rate of change slowed. Now that the immediate actions had been taken, he was waiting for the officer of the deck (OOD) to order supplemental actions.

Now, *now*, I thought. The downward pitch had essentially been arrested, the speed was coming off smartly, and the downward depth rate was minimal. Now was the time to vent the forward ballast tanks and go to "all stop" on the main engines. If the backing bell were left on too long, the ship would actually start going backward through the water, which was undesirable.

The OOD was looking around nervously. This wasn't a good sign. During casualties, I would watch the eyes of the watch officer. If they went down, bad. If they went to a written procedure, bad. If they looked unfocused, bad. If they were focused on the indications that would provide the necessary information for him to make the next decision, good.

Inexperienced officers almost always waited too long right at this point in the emergency. They wanted to see an upward depth rate before venting. By that time it would be too late; the expanding air would create more and more positive buoyancy forward that couldn't be vented out fast enough, and we'd be pitching up at a steep angle, still out of control.

If the OOD didn't order the venting within the next few seconds, the drill monitor would step in and the drill would be a failure. I was sorely tempted to shine my flashlight on the vent switches to help out, but resisted.

The chief of the watch (COW), YN1 Scott Dillon, placed his hand on the forward vent switch. The OOD noticed the movement. . . .

"COW, vent the forward group, helm, all stop."

"Vent the forward group."

"All stop."

"Forward vents open."

"Maneuvering answers all stop."

Yes, that was it. Perfect. The ship slowed to a near hover and leveled out.

The COW's action to point to the vent switch, the next key action, was critical to this success.

I asked Dillon, "Why did you do that?"

Well, he explained, he knew it was the next action to take, and with deliberate action, he wanted to be ready for the order.

Yes, and at the same time he signaled to the OOD in a tense time, without injecting more words, what the OOD needed to order.

In this way, we learned another powerful aspect of deliberate action: think about it as anticipatory deliberate action. With the movements of watch standers indicating the next action they anticipate taking, they signal fellow team members and supervisors what they should be thinking about. It was powerful and helpful.

Thereafter, whenever we talked about deliberate action, we talked about multiple benefits. Not only did it minimize the chance of a mistake by a person by himself and provide an opportunity for drill team intervention; it was also a critical aspect of teamwork. It worked in a couple ways. It was a bottom-up way of signaling action. It also worked because adjacent watch standers could correct potential mistakes before they happened. This was an excellent example of putting our mechanism of deliberate action into practice.

Mechanism: Use Your Legacy for Inspiration

After recovering from the drill, *Santa Fe* continued transiting south through the South China Sea. We were being vectored toward the Arabian Sea through the Strait of Malacca. I headed back to the engine room to work out on the exercise bike. (After all, I had my own personal goals like everyone else.)

A few minutes later I heard "Attention to port." It was the OOD, Lieutenant Dave Adams, on the 1MC.

That was highly unusual. I'd never heard "attention to port," starboard, or anything on the 1MC before. I got off the bike.

"We are now passing the approximate location of where the USS *Grayling* was sunk in September 1943."

A few moments later, "Carry on."

Wow, what a great idea. *Grayling* was one of the fifty-two American submarines that were sunk in World War II. As we operated in the western Pacific, we would occasionally chance past the location of one of those lost submarines. Some of the locations were known precisely, but in some cases, like the *Grayling*, the exact date and location remain a mystery. What we do know is that *Grayling* delivered supplies to guerrilla fighters at Pandan Bay, Panay, on the west coast of the Philippines on August 23, 1943. After that it departed to hunt for Japanese merchant ships off Manila. The Navy estimated the time and location of its sinking based on postwar Japanese records and radio communications.[7]

As submariners, we have a tremendous legacy, but no formal program for inspiring a crew with that legacy. On board *Santa Fe*, we adopted several practices that would connect us to this rich legacy and educate the new members of the crew about what the submarine force had accomplished during World War II. We'd post notes in the Plan of the Day (POD) and read Medal of Honor or battle citations whenever we qualified a member of *Santa Fe* in submarines. We would make announcements when passing sunken submarines. Back in Pearl Harbor, we visited the USS *Bowfin* submarine museum and called it officer training.

I was worried that the crew would think some of these things tacky, but that wasn't the case. It helped provide organizational clarity into what we were about—the why for our service.

USE YOUR LEGACY FOR INSPIRATION is a mechanism for CLARITY.

Many organizations have inspiring early starts and somehow

"lose their way" at some later point. I urge you to tap into the sense of purpose and urgency that developed during those early days or during some crisis. The trick is to find real ways to keep those alive as the organization grows. One of the easiest is simply to talk about them. Embed them into your guiding principles and use those words in efficiency reports and personnel awards.

In the submarine force, we had an obvious, unselfish, and rich legacy of service to the country, but we were almost embarrassed to talk about it. I'm not espousing an unthinking "kill bad guys" culture, but that wasn't what happened. We just needed to resurrect the true legacy of our predecessors.

Later, Rear Admiral Al Konetzni invited me to Washington, D.C., to represent the Pacific Submarine Force at a large convention with the Department of Defense and submarine industry leaders. A significant number of retired admirals were in the audience. I decided to use this theme and titled the speech "The Spirit Is Alive." I simply talked about how the young sailors in today's Navy understood and appreciated what had happened before us, and in our way, we were doing our best to be true to that legacy. It was a great success and brought the crowd to a standing ovation that lasted a long time.

QUESTIONS TO CONSIDER

- What is the legacy of your organization?
- How does that legacy shed light on your organization's purpose?
- What kind of actions can you take to bring this legacy alive for individuals in your organization?

23

Leadership at Every Level

Do your guiding principles help people in your organization make decisions? We figured out a way to do just that.

1998 (a year before taking command of *Santa Fe*), Newport, Rhode Island, Command Leadership School

"Commander Marquet, could you come see me?" I was being summoned for counseling.

Command Leadership School had been a welcome two-week sabbatical during the yearlong PCO training. There were readings, discussions, and a couple of exercises. One of the exercises had been for everyone to write the guiding principles for their command to implement upon their arrival. I turned in a blank piece of paper.

"Are you aware that you turned in a blank sheet?"

"Yes sir, I am."

"Well, don't you think that you as the commander have an obligation to create a vision for your command?" It was more of a statement than a question.

"No, I feel that my job as the commander is to tap into the existing energy of the command, discover the strengths, and remove barriers to further progress."

The class supervisor looked at me as if I had three heads, but I knew he wasn't going to fail me.

When I first got to *Santa Fe*, I sent out a survey asking the officers and chiefs what they thought the strengths of the command were and what our guiding principles should be. We then had a couple of meetings to select the few we wanted to keep (constraint: they all had to fit on one page) and what they meant. We were so busy, however, getting the ship out for the first underway and inspection and then the repair period, we hadn't done much other than collect the initial inputs.

Now, on deployment, we had the time to finish the job of defining our guiding principles.

The chiefs gathered in the wardroom one evening and the officers the next. I wanted to make the guiding principles real, not something that just hung on the wall somewhere. When thinking about the principles and their utility, I used this question: If I were a crew member and faced with deciding between two different courses of action, would these principles provide me with the right criteria against which to select the appropriate course of action?

The guiding principles needed to do just that: provide guidance on decisions.

USS *Santa Fe* Guiding Principles

Initiative
Initiative means we take action without direction from above to improve our knowledge as submariners, prepare the command for its mission, and come up with solutions to problems. With

each member of the command taking initiative, the leverage is immense. Initiative has been a hallmark of the American fighting man and a key reason for our success. Initiative places an obligation on the chain of command not to stifle initiative in subordinates.

Innovation

Innovation means looking at new ways of doing the same thing. It also means knowing which areas are "above the waterline" and appropriate to innovation, having the courage to change, and tolerating failures.

Intimate Technical Knowledge

Modern submarines are extremely complex. Intimate technical knowledge means that each of us is responsible for learning our area of responsibility. We make decisions based on technical reasons, not hope. We understand the details of our watch stations and the interrelationship of systems. We diligently study.

Courage

Courage means we choose to do the right thing, even if it may be uncomfortable. It means not just doing or saying what subordinates, peers, or superiors want to see or hear. It means admitting mistakes, even if ugly.

Commitment

Commitment means we are present when we come to work. We give it our best. We choose to be here.

Continuous Improvement

Continuous improvement is how we get better. We continually seek ways to learn from processes and improve them and ourselves. The chain of command has the obligation to develop and institute mechanisms (such as conducting debriefs) to achieve continuous improvement.

Integrity

Integrity means we tell the truth to each other and to ourselves. It means we have a grounded base of reality and see things as they are, not as we want them to be. Integrity means we participate fully in debriefs, allowing improvements to be based on facts.

Empowerment

We encourage those below us to take action and support them if they make mistakes. We employ stewardship delegation, explaining what we want accomplished and allow flexibility in how it is accomplished.

Teamwork

Submariners have traditionally worked as a team because a mistake by one person can mean disaster for all. We work as a team, not undercutting each other. The chain of command is obligated to implement mechanisms that encourage and reward teamwork. We back each other up in a positive way.

Openness

We exercise participative openness: freedom to speak one's mind. Additionally, we exercise reflective openness, which leads to looking inward. We challenge our own thinking. We avoid the trap of listening to refute.

Timeliness

Timeliness means we do things on time: start work on time, qualify on time, are ready to start evolutions and drills on time, and get to rendezvous points on time. Timeliness also recognizes that accomplishing most things faster is better and that working to reduce inherent delays and time lags results in a more effective organization.

Leadership at Every Level!

Mechanism: Use Guiding Principles for Decision Criteria

Leaders like to hang a list of guiding principles on office walls for display, but often those principles don't become part of the fabric of the organization. Not on *Santa Fe*. We did several things to reinforce these principles and make them real to the crew. For example, when we wrote awards or evaluations, we tried to couch behaviors in the language of these principles. "Petty Officer M exhibited Courage and Openness when reporting . . ."

My own behavior frequently needed adjustment when it was tested against the guiding principles. For example, I might initially attempt to dismiss a sailor who had a suggestion for a new way of doing business without listening to his suggestion. I might be expecting openness from the sailors but at the same time responding to reports of mistakes with short-tempered irritation rather than reflective curiosity. When the guiding principles were helping me, they were likely helping others.

Guiding principles have to accurately represent the principles of the real organization, not the imagined organization. Falseness in what the organization is about results in problems. Since these are a set of criteria that employees will use when they make decisions, decisions won't be aligned to the organization's goals.

I have seen this, for instance, in an organization that talked about safety first but whose real interests were in profits and accepting degradations in safety if they seemed "reasonable." After all, the safest thing to do is to shut down and send everyone home. But not acknowledging that they would be balancing safety with profits resulted in miscommunication, lack of credibility (because everyone knew the truth), and unaligned decisions.

USE GUIDING PRINCIPLES FOR DECISION CRITERIA is a mechanism for CLARITY.

Most of you have organizational principles. Go out and ask the first three people you see what they are. I was at one organization that proudly displayed its motto in Latin. I asked everyone I saw what it meant. The only one who knew was the CEO. That's not good.

QUESTIONS TO CONSIDER

- How can you simplify your guiding principles so that everyone in your organization understands them?
- How will you communicate your principles to others?
- Are your guiding principles referenced in evaluations and performance awards?
- Are your guiding principles useful to employees as decision-making criteria?
- Do your guiding principles serve as decision-making criteria for your people?
- Do you know your own guiding principles? Do others know them?

24

A Dangerous Passage

Do you recognize your staff's achievements so long after the event that even they forget? We learned not to let admin get in the way.

July 10, 1999: The Strait of Malacca

Santa Fe was on the surface transiting westward through the Strait of Malacca. It's a tough transit. More than 160 large vessels—nearly half the world's oil tankers—pass through the strait every day.[8] Because it is shallow, any submarine must transit on the surface, an unnatural and uncomfortable place to be. After all, a submarine is designed not to be seen, and our speed is slower on the surface than it is when submerged.

Near Singapore, ferries and tugs with tows create significant cross-traffic between Singapore and Indonesia. Finally, the gap between the east- and westbound maritime traffic lanes was full of small fishing boats—sometimes no larger than a paddleboard—that wandered into the main traffic lane from time to time.

Our plan for making the difficult three-day passage was to

tuck in one thousand yards behind one of the large westbound (empty) oil tankers and draft in its shadow like a cyclist in the Tour de France. Ships would avoid the large, easy-to-see tanker, and we'd get a clear path. The trick was to get close enough not to let the other traffic close in behind the tanker but at the same time maintain a safe distance. I split the time with my new XO, Lieutenant Commander Tom Stanley, on the bridge. I'd be up there for twelve hours, then he would drive the ship. I took the night shift.

On the first night, as we were passing the lights of Singapore to our starboard, I noticed a dim light moving across us.

While I was trying to figure out what it meant, Rick Panlilio, the OOD, shouted, "All back emergency, right hard rudder!"

Immediately the ship started shuddering as the throttleman back in maneuvering shut the ahead throttles and rapidly opened the astern throttles, reversing the main engines and *Santa Fe*'s screw. The light was a dimly lit tugboat, and the tug was on one side of our path and its tow on the other.

We barely stopped short of the towline between the tug and the barge. I was shaken.

I came down off the bridge and went directly to maneuvering to applaud the efforts of the engineering team. The petty officer who had "pushed the red tag" aside in the shore power incident was the throttleman. He had spared us from a collision. It was 0515 and the watch team was about to get relieved. I grabbed YN1 Scott Dillon, who maintained the supply of awards, and asked him to get me a Navy Achievement Medal. With it, I returned to the crew's mess and pinned it on the throttleman while he and the off-going watch team ate breakfast. I spoke words of appreciation and professionalism. Later, I would formally report his exemplary service, but the immediacy of the recognition was important.

Mechanism: Use Immediate Recognition to
Reinforce Desired Behaviors

We let our administrative processes get in the way of prompt recognition. Many times we would submit awards three months prior to the departure of a sailor, only to find ourselves calling during the last week to track down the award before his departure. When I say immediate recognition, I mean immediate. Not thirty days. Not thirty minutes. Immediate.

Look at your structures for awards. Are they limited? Do they pit some of your employees against others? That structure will result in competition at the lowest level. If what you want is collaboration, then you are destroying it.

Instead, have awards that are abundant, with no limit. They pit your team against the world—either external competitors or nature. I like to call these man-versus-nature as opposed to man-versus-man awards. Every team that can get a fire hose to the scene of the fire within two minutes gets an award (the "award" could be a superior grade). In cases where there is a physical reason for the goal, this is better than, say, having the top 10 percent of the shortest times get an "excellent." On the one hand, it's possible that the best times are three minutes, and you are handing out "excellents" to a team that would actually die in a fire. On the other hand, once the team has gotten better than two minutes, you don't need them to spend more time and energy honing that skill. Better to move to another problem area.

The most important change that happens, however, is that all teams (in our case, all submarines) are now collaborators working against a common external goal as opposed to competitors working against one another. One of the things I tried to change was the collaboration-competition boundary. When I got to *Santa Fe*, people within the ship were competing with one another: department heads for the top fitness report (fitrep) spot, nukes against supply for blame on who didn't order the part, and so on.

We deliberately pushed that boundary to the skin of the ship. We'd say "There is no 'they' on *Santa Fe*." We wanted cooperation within the ship and the competition to be against the other submarines or, better yet, the potential enemy.

USE IMMEDIATE RECOGNITION TO REINFORCE DESIRED BEHAVIORS is a mechanism for CLARITY.

Some people worry that having a fixed objective reduces the incentive for continuous improvement and breeds a mentality that "we just need to meet the goal." In some cases, this is appropriate, but in other cases, relative grading is also appropriate. There's no reason you can't do both: assign the grade based on the fixed objective and provide data on how that team stacks up against all teams.

Simply providing data to the teams on their relative performance results in a natural desire to improve. This has been called "gamification." The blog to read more about this is Gabe Zichermann's *Gamification* blog: www.gamification.co.

QUESTIONS TO CONSIDER

- Do you have a recognition and rewards system in place that allows you to immediately applaud top performers?
- How can you create scoring systems that immediately reward employees for the behaviors you want?
- Have you seen evidence of "gamification" in your workplace? Perhaps it's worth reading one of Gabe Zichermann's blog posts and discussing it with your management team.

Looking Ahead

Are you mired in short-term thinking? For me it was tough to start thinking beyond the next inspection, but it paid off.

July 15, 1999: Indian Ocean

I mentioned that we deployed two weeks earlier than originally scheduled. We were able to accomplish that because of a conversation I had with Lieutenant Dave Adams about three months prior. At the time, we were on track to be ready for deployment. The crew was adapting well to the many changes we'd made, and he earnestly wanted to get them some time off before we left our families behind for the six-month deployment. We were scheduled to depart for the western Pacific and the Arabian Gulf on June 29. In that time, we had myriad things to fix and equipment to load, including missiles and torpedoes, all of which had to be checked. We were also scheduled to return to San Diego for a second set of battle group exercises, a tactical inspection, and the final certification for our deployment.

I appreciated what Weps was saying. In the scheduling books, all ships showed a predeployment "stand-down" in the two weeks prior to deployment, but it was effectively just an accounting tool so the staff could say the ship had stand-down. In reality, that period was crammed with frenetic activity and no one had any time off.

By beginning with the end in mind, however, we should be able to do something about negotiating at least part of that stand-down period for the crew. Following up on Dave's goal, we got the department heads and chiefs together and looked at the schedule.

The only way we would be able to give the crew two weeks off in June, just before we deployed, would be if we were completely *ready* for deployment two weeks early. This would be tough because the external organizations—the weapons loading facility and the Pearl Harbor Naval Shipyard—would know they actually had another two weeks to finalize preparations and work would "slip" into that period.

Internally, the department heads would need to have the ship ready in all respects on June 8, a full three weeks before the scheduled deployment date. I would personally approve all exceptions for any work planned after that date. It would be a tall order and was met with groans of impossibility. Against that backdrop, however, we talked about what would be achieved: a true stand-down where we could spend time with our families before the six-month deployment. It was my job to notify external parties—the squadron and the repair facility, primarily—that we had drawn a line in the sand and *Santa Fe* needed to be ready in all respects on June 8.

We put the word out to the crew and started figuring out how to be ready on our target date.

Then, at the end of April, with about six weeks to go, Commodore Mark Kenny called me. The nation needed us to deploy eleven days early, on June 18. Well, we could and we did. It was only because we were already working on our plan for being ready three weeks early that it was possible. Unfortunately, we did lose much of the family time we'd hoped for. We would have a short stand-down; the nation needed us and we would deliver.

Mechanism: Begin with the End in Mind*

We had started a new practice. Now, I wanted to build on the success of that practice. I decided that one key supervisor a day, rotating among the XO, COB, Weps, Nav, Eng, and Suppo, would have an hour-long mentoring session with me. The rule for the mentoring meeting was that we could talk only about long-term issues, and primarily people issues. All business concerning a leaking valve or failed circuit card had to occur outside these meetings.

During the first set of discussions, we adapted a useful technique for long-term focus and planning. I asked each of them to write their end-of-tour awards. Since these supervisors are assigned to the submarine for three years, this particular exercise made them look that far into the future. If someone was having trouble visualizing that far out I asked him to write his performance evaluation for the next year. Lieutenant Commander Bill Greene would be transferring in a few months, but Lieutenant Commander Tom Stanley, Lieutenant Dave Adams, and Lieutenant Commander Rick Panlilio weren't leaving for another two years. I wanted this to be a serious exercise; I wouldn't let them turn in a quick response. I assigned it as homework between two mentoring sessions a week apart. Then we would look at the write-up together.

When we looked at Dave's end-of-tour award write-up, I noted he had some great ideas. It struck me that I had entered this mentoring practice with the idea of a traditional mentor-mentee relationship and hadn't realized the incompatibility of that

---

* The phrase comes from Stephen Covey's *The 7 Habits of Highly Effective People*.

hierarchy with leader-leader. I learned as much from them as they did from me. Hence, we were practicing a mentor-mentor program.

Dave and I discussed each one of his goals and made it as specific and measurable as possible. Dave made a plan to accomplish each of the things in the write-up, spaced over the next two years. He was going to get two fitness reports (fitreps) over those two years as well, and we applied the same approach to the fitreps, making goals measurable and setting in place the tools to collect the data.

Two years later, when Dave transferred off *Santa Fe*, his department had accomplished almost everything he'd written down, and the actual citation sounded just like our vision.

Frequently, we would start off by writing about achieving certain levels of qualification, as in "qualify for command," or having general goals for their team, such as "have my department do better in procedural compliance." Objectives like these are too vague and hard to quantify, so we would work to write the objective in measurable ways. We'd arrive at the specifics by asking a question such as:

"How would you know if procedural compliance was improved?"

"We'd have fewer critiques."

"Okay. How many fewer? How many did you have last year?"

"Don't know, didn't count."

In this way, we generated verifiable measures. And in the process, we often learned that we hadn't been keeping track of the appropriate data, and we'd have to start doing so.

The Navy's performance system is deliberately constructed to make the highest comparative rankings scarce. Since we had three department heads and one XO on *Santa Fe* who were all of the rank lieutenant or lieutenant commander, they were competing against one another. As a result, it is difficult to get all of them promoted because only one will get the top recommendation. We were able to get everyone promoted and had tremendous success with bigger groups like the first class petty officer evaluations as well.

Customarily, selection boards read performance evaluations that are filled with phrases like "significantly improved procedural compliance," which are basically meaningless. The evaluations of the officers on *Santa Fe*, on the other hand, would report "reduced critiques by 43 percent, reduced percent of the crew smoking by 12 percent, increased on-time performance by 31 percent," and so on. I believe the ability to specifically quantify accomplishments, in addition to the focus this exercise required of the officers and the overall reputation of the ship, went a long way toward allowing us to boast disproportionately high selection rates. During my last year in command, 2001, we had ten men eligible to be promoted from first class petty officer to chief petty officer. We had an amazing 90 percent selection rate, promoting nine chiefs. In one day the number of chiefs almost doubled (and then they transferred to other boats). It was gratifying to see YN1 Scott Dillon, whom I met as a second class petty officer when I reported on board, make chief. Using hard data was an effective way of proving we had achieved the end we had in mind.

How to Begin with the End in Mind

Here are some things you can do to "begin with the end in mind":

- Hand out this chapter as reading material. Also consider Stephen Covey's *The 7 Habits of Highly Effective People*, chapter 2, "Begin with the End in Mind."
- Discuss the concepts and idea of "Begin with the end in mind."
- With your leadership team, develop longer-term organizational goals for three to five years out.
- Go through the evaluations and look for statements that express achievement. In every case, ask "How would we know?" and ensure that you have measuring systems in place.

- Then have employees write their own evaluations one year, two years, or three years hence. The goals in the employees' evaluations should cascade down from the organization's goals; they needn't necessarily be identical but they should be appropriate at an individual level.
- Have conversations with employees to make their desired achievements indisputable (How would I know?) and measurable.

While the end-of-tour awards write-up exercise was beneficial because it forced each officer to get clear in his own mind what he wanted to achieve, it also opened the way to helpful dialogue. In my dialogues with each supervisor, I discussed what I was trying to accomplish on *Santa Fe,* and collectively they were able to translate that to what they needed to accomplish within their departments in order to support the higher-level goals. These discussions, during which we talked at length about the recursive goals and accomplishments, were very beneficial. BEGIN WITH THE END IN MIND is an important mechanism for ORGANIZATIONAL CLARITY.

As you work with individuals in your organization to develop their vision for the future, it is crucial that you establish specific, measurable goals. These goals will help the individuals realize their ambitions. In addition, you as a mentor have to establish that you are sincerely interested in the problems of the person you are mentoring. By taking action to support the individual, you will prove that you are indeed working in their best interest and always keeping the end in mind.

QUESTIONS TO CONSIDER

- For how far in the future are you optimizing your organization?
- Are you mentoring solely to instruct or also to learn?

- Will you know if you've accomplished your organizational and personal goals?
- Are you measuring the things you need to be?
- Have you assigned a team to write up the company's goals three to five years out?
- What will it take to redesign your management team's schedule so you can mentor one another?
- How can you reward staff members who attain their measurable goals?

Combat Effectiveness

Are you looking for resilience in your organization? We realized that resilience and effectiveness sometimes meant questioning orders.

September 1999: Somewhere in the Arabian Gulf

"Up scope."

In the shallow water of the Arabian Gulf, we were setting up an attack on another submarine—the USS *Olympia*, which was playing an enemy diesel boat. We were halfway through our deployment period and were about to shoot the first-ever submarine-launched torpedo in the Arabian Gulf. It was an exercise and the target was Oly. (This was the submarine I was originally ordered to command, you might recall.)

We had the Commander, Submarine Group Seven, Rear Admiral Joseph Krol, on board to observe the exercise. Admiral Krol had allowed me to send Rick Panlilio home for the birth of his child and approved the early swap of Lieutenant Commander Tom Stanley as XO. It would be important to show the admiral he'd made the right decision. The pressure was on. This was going to be the test of leader-leader versus leader-follower. Would the mechanisms I had put in place deliver the kind of results I hoped for?

We were in position and I was sure no one would be asking to raise the communications mast this time. So far, so good. Just like the Maui basin, the water in the Arabian Gulf is shallow, and we needed to be in a good tactical position. We were demonstrating not only the capabilities of the USS *Santa Fe*, but more important, the U.S. submarine force's ability to attack and sink submarines in this shallow body of water. We wanted any potential adversaries to know that they weren't safe here or anywhere, and instead of making speeches, we were demonstrating it.

"Target, bearing . . . MARK." Lieutenant Commander Rick Panlilio was on the scope and saw the "enemy."

"Down scope."

Lieutenant Commander Tom Stanley, the XO, announced that we had a firing solution, and Lieutenant Dave Adams recommended we shoot.

I didn't have to drive the problem and was able to sit back and absorb the whole scene, walking from station to station, looking at the faces and posture of the men in the fire control party.

I ordered, "Shoot tube three."

A shudder, and the exercise torpedo was on its way.

"Torpedo running hot, straight, and normal" was Weps's report.

Officially, we were supposed to say, "Wire clearance maneuver complete, torpedo running." But we'd changed our language to match what the World War II submariners said. Again, this was an example of our mechanism to tap our rich heritage.

I looked over at Admiral Krol and he seemed to be enjoying himself—a good sign.

The exercise torpedo signaled a hit! I announced it on the 1MC to cheers. The torpedo would now surface and a supporting craft with a crane would haul it out of the water and back to shore for refurbishment.

I headed down to the crew's mess for a cup of coffee. The mess was packed with damage control parties conducting training. Admiral Krol came down and presided over a reenlistment ceremony. Since we were in a combat zone, the bonuses we awarded sailors when they reenlisted were tax-free. Ultimately, we would reenlist thirty-six sailors in 1999, twelve times the number who reenlisted in 1998. I would award more than half a million dollars in reenlistment bonuses, a record then. Leader-leader had paid off again.

December 1999: Somewhere in the Pacific

"Yellow sounding" was announced over the ship's loudspeaker.

I was walking the ship with my flashlight and bolted for the control room. It was 0300, and we were carefully positioned to pick up a SEAL team coming out from land nearby. It had taken a lot to get to this point, and now we were about to muck it all up. Yellow sounding meant the water depth was less than we'd planned and we needed to move.

It was nearly a year into my tour as the captain of *Santa Fe*. We were back from deployment and conducting an exercise with the SEALs. We were in the last of three phases.

For phase one, we rendezvoused with a helicopter and picked up the SEAL team. Eleven burly guys, their weapons, two rolled-up Zodiac inflatable boats, two motors for the Zodiacs, and a bunch of equipment to blow stuff up left the helicopter, came on board the submarine, and went down the hatch. The helicopter flew away. Total elapsed time: less than a minute.

Together with the SEAL team we planned the mission for phase two. We transited near the location and scoped it out. We noticed where the shore lights were, where the fishing boats were, and—more important—where they weren't. We checked local currents and the angle of the moon at various times in the night. After finding a good drop-off and recover point, we surfaced at night and launched the SEALs toward the beach. That had been three days earlier.

Now, it was time to pick them up, phase three. I imagined being one of those SEALs: having successfully accomplished the mission, getting back into the Zodiac, and heading out into the ocean in the middle of the night, hoping to find the submarine. Even though this was an exercise, the ocean was real, the near-empty gas tanks were real, and the darkness was real. It was important that we were in position for these guys.

It was pitch-black in the control room; we wanted to keep it dark inside so that the periscope operator could see outside. The speakers from our early warning receiver were chirping away. These are pulses from other radars that are being intercepted by our equipment and are translated to this audible tone. By the characteristics of the chirps—regular, of a certain tone—I could tell they were indicating regular fishing boats and merchants in the distance. Nothing to worry about.

Reports were coming into the control room from different parts of the ship: readiness to pick up the SEALs; the status of other contacts also confirmed we were all set. Things seemed to be going well.

I passed through the crew's mess, one deck below the control room. Here, the lights were on and blankets were stacked in piles in case they were needed. Even though it was three o'clock in the morning, the crew was still ready to serve these guys soup as soon as they arrived on board.

Aft of the crew's mess is the escape trunk. This is the main hatch that we would open to allow the SEALs to come down into the ship. This is where we would triage any injured SEALs.

Beyond that, I passed into the engine room where the nukes were ready to provide maximum propulsion even though we were sitting at all stop right now on the surface. The nuclear reactor was still running to provide us electric power and steam in case we needed it. If something happened—if a patrol craft or an enemy airplane came by, and we had to make a choice between getting out of there and leaving the SEALs or saving the ship—we were going to save the ship. It was important to plan, to pick the right location.

Forward, in the lowest level, in the torpedo room, torpedoes were loaded and ready. We didn't expect trouble, but we were prepared to face it.

The wardroom, where the officers eat, was set up like an operating room by Doc Hill. This was where he would deal with any injured SEALs.

Now, here's the thing: almost none of these preparations had happened because of my orders. They happened because someone on the crew thought, "Hey, those guys are going to be wet. They're going to be cold. They're going to be hungry. They might be injured. And we should get ready for them." My crew didn't wait for orders. They just did what needed to be done and informed the appropriate personnel. It was leader-leader all the way.

That's when the yellow sounding was announced.

Mechanism: Encourage a Questioning Attitude over Blind Obedience

I entered the control room, where things were strangely calm. Surely my guys knew that if we moved out of position it would make it much harder for us to find the SEALs and for them to find us. The OOD on the bridge had already ordered "Ahead one third."

I looked at the digital chart. A little arrow indicated our direction of motion, and it was pointing slightly toward the beach. I thought, "We don't want to go ahead, we need to back out." So I shouted out, "That's wrong. We need to back." (This meant order a backing bell.)

In the darkness, we recognized each other's voices. Sled Dog was standing quartermaster. There was a pause and silence for half a second, then he said frankly, "No, Captain, you're wrong."

It stunned me, and I shut up and just started looking at the indications in the control room, including the compass repeaters showing the heading of the ship. I thought about what it takes for a young sailor to say, "Captain, you're wrong."

It dawned on me. The bow was pointing *away* from land and

we were being set astern. That was what the arrow on the digital chart was showing. And I remembered that the watch team had planned it this way, with the bow out, in case we needed to make a quick getaway.

The small arrow shrank and grew in the direction away from land. The OOD ordered all stop. We'd moved one hundred yards, but that was all it took to reach deeper water.

Moments later we saw the Zodiacs. Had the men followed my order, we would have gone in the wrong direction; we might have missed them.

As I write this, the news is filled with the tragedy in Italy. On January 13, 2012, the cruise ship *Costa Concordia* ran aground off Isola del Giglio. It appears the captain ordered a course deviation to take the ship close to the island as a nautical tribute to one of the employees. I wonder if anyone spoke up. How about the officer of the deck? How about the second in command? How about the helmsman, who must have seen the lights of the island less than a mile away? I sure wish some of them had had a questioning attitude. ENCOURAGE A QUESTIONING ATTITUDE OVER BLIND OBEDIENCE is a mechanism for CLARITY.

QUESTIONS TO CONSIDER

- How do we create resilient organizations where errors are stopped as opposed to propagating through the system?
- Will your people follow an order that isn't correct?
- Do you want obedience or effectiveness?
- Have you built a culture that embraces a questioning attitude?

Homecoming

Do you have the fortitude to go against the grain? There are significant benefits to thinking differently about leadership.

January 2000: At Anchor off Lahaina, Maui

We were thrilled to get back from deployment before Christmas and be reunited with our families. After the holidays, we got under way for a short period in the Hawaiian Islands for proficiency training. I had already been using some of Dr. Stephen Covey's material from *7 Habits*, so when he expressed a desire to ride a submarine, it was a natural fit for him to come ride *Santa Fe*. During his visit on board the *Santa Fe*, Dr. Covey asked me what the ship had accomplished. I ticked off the following list of accomplishments:

- We steamed forty thousand miles safely.
- We made nine port calls in six different countries, and the crew had acted as perfect ambassadors.
- We hadn't had a single liberty incident, something that I

was reminded to avoid by my various bosses prior to the arrival of every port visit.

- We maintained the submarine at 100 percent operational readiness, with zero operational impact due to repair, maintenance, personnel, or any other issue.
- While on deployment, we reenlisted nineteen crew members for a total of more than half a million dollars in reenlistment bonuses, a record at the time.
- We awarded 22 submarine qualifications (dolphins), and the crew qualified 290 individual watch stations, an average of 2.4 qualifications for each crew member.
- Operationally, we had demonstrated some key capabilities, including our torpedo exercise in the Arabian Gulf, transiting the Strait of Hormuz several times and the Strait of Malacca twice, and picking up the U.S. Navy SEALs.

Of course, there were some things I couldn't tell him about. To my mind, the most impressive statistic was the improvement in our retention results. The numbers came out like this:

CATEGORY	1998	1999
Enlisted reenlistments	3	36
Officer retention	0%	100%
Enlisted personnel selected for officer programs	1	3
Enlisted personnel advanced	30	48
Personnel determined to be ineligible for reenlistment (a bad thing)	8	1
Weeks (average) to qualify in submarines	45	38
Enlisted contact coordinators	1	8
E6 qualified diving officers	0	2
Port/starboard watch stations	7	0

CATEGORY	1998	1999
Engineering assessment	Below average	Above average
Training program effectiveness	"Not effective"	"Very effective"
Medical assessment	Worst of 6 in Squadron Seven	Best of 6 in Squadron Seven
Contact coordination	Below average	Excellent
Tactical effectiveness in various mission areas	Below average to average	Above average to excellent

Why had the retention numbers gone up so much? Well, there were a number of reasons, but one of the key ones was that the junior enlisted men used to look to see what their chiefs did to get a sense of whether they wanted to stick around and have that job. The old-school chiefs didn't have a particularly hard life, emphasizing the privilege of rank over obligation, but it wasn't relevant. They weren't in charge of anything.

With the concept of Chiefs in Charge, the chiefs were working twice as hard. They needed to be out and about, being in charge of evolutions and ensuring that things went properly. They were the ones standing in front of the CO explaining why things hadn't gone as well as they should have. Yet, their jobs now mattered and the decisions they made—they actually had decisions to make—affected the lives of 135 sailors and the combat effectiveness of a $2 billion warship. This was a job people could sign up for.

Two junior officers withdrew their resignation requests.

Santa Fe was awarded the Arleigh Burke Fleet Trophy. This award is given to the submarine, ship, or aircraft squadron having achieved the greatest improvement in battle efficiency during the calendar year. I attribute this to the leader-leader structure we developed on board *Santa Fe.*

Dr. Covey told me it was the most empowered organization he'd seen anywhere, not just in the military. (I was gratified to receive this recognition from a man whose work we had used to get us there.) Unfettered by the mental image of leader-follower, the crew approached the business of making every evolution, every operation excellent. At the time, we knew we were developing something new, but we didn't know what it was. Through trial and error, the crew arrived at a body of practices and principles that were dramatically more effective than those within the leader-follower model. It was only toward the end that we understood we had replaced the leader-follower model with the leader-leader model.

I continued to see benefits of deliberate action. DELIBERATE first of all reduced errors by operators and was also a mechanism for TEAMWORK. Finally, it was a mechanism for SIGNALING INTENT.

A year later, at the beginning of 2001, we received the highest grade anyone had ever seen on our reactor operations examination, with top marks in every area. Afterward I talked with the senior inspector, a captain. He told me that my guys tried to make as many mistakes as the average ship. The difference was that the mistakes never happened because of deliberate action.

I didn't know it at the time, but the power of leader-leader was just starting to kick in.

We had accomplished numerous other breakthroughs as well:

- Instead of focusing on intimate review of the work, I focused on intimate review of the people.
- Instead of requiring more reports and more inspection points, I required fewer.
- Instead of more "leadership" resulting in more "follower-ship," I practiced less leadership, resulting in more leadership at every level of the command.

After Dr. Covey's visit, I thought long and hard about the mechanisms we had put in place and how they worked together. I was struck that it seemed in many cases we were doing the opposite of what traditional leadership would have had us do. Here are some examples:

DON'T DO THIS!	DO THIS!
Leader-follower	Leader-leader
Take control	Give control
Give orders	Avoid giving orders
When you give orders, be confident, unambiguous, and resolute	When you do give orders, leave room for questioning
Brief	Certify
Have meetings	Have conversations
Have a mentor-mentee program	Have a mentor-mentor program
Focus on technology	Focus on people
Think short-term	Think long-term
Want to be missed after you depart	Want not to be missed after you depart
Have high-repetition, low-quality training	Have low-repetition, high-quality training
Limit communications to terse, succinct, formal orders	Augment orders with rich, contextual, informal communications
Be questioning	Be curious
Make inefficient processes efficient	Eliminate entire steps and processes that don't add value
Increase monitoring and inspection points	Reduce monitoring and inspection points
Protect information	Pass information

Additionally, we formulated the overall construct presented here: control, competence, and clarity. Up to this point we had been just "doing stuff" and seeing what worked and what didn't. I can't claim a predetermined plan, other than a vague notion that we needed to get everyone's full mental capacity, creativity, and energy involved.

The mechanisms fit under the three keys in the following way.

Instituting the Leader-Leader Model

The core of the leader-leader model is giving employees *control* over what they work on and how they work. It means letting them make meaningful decisions. The two enabling pillars are *competence* and *clarity*. Here is a listing of the mechanisms outlined in this book:

Control
- Find the genetic code for control and rewrite it.
- Act your way to new thinking.
- Short, early conversations make efficient work.
- Use "I intend to . . ." to turn passive followers into active leaders.
- Resist the urge to provide solutions.
- Eliminate top-down monitoring systems.
- Think out loud (both superiors and subordinates).
- Embrace the inspectors.

Competence
- Take deliberate action.
- We learn (everywhere, all the time).
- Don't brief, certify.
- Continually and consistently repeat the message.
- Specify goals, not methods.

Clarity
- Achieve excellence, don't just avoid errors.
- Build trust and take care of your people.

- Use your legacy for inspiration.
- Use guiding principles for decision criteria.
- Use immediate recognition to reinforce desired behaviors.
- Begin with the end in mind.
- Encourage a questioning attitude over blind obedience.

It's my hope that this organization of the mechanisms in this book will help you put these ideas into action as you adopt the leader-leader philosophy.

Here's a summary of the exercise I take organizations through when they want to move in the direction of leader-leader.

First, identify where excellence is created in your company. There may be some internal processes that generate excellence and there may be some interface processes that generate excellence. Generally I find that interfaces with the customer and with the physical world are two key interfaces. Then, figure out what decisions the people responsible for the interfaces need to make in order to achieve excellence. Finally, understand what it would take to get those employees to be able to make those decisions. This typically requires an intersection of the right technical knowledge, a thorough understanding of your organization's goals, authority to make the decision, and responsibility for the consequences of the decisions made.

QUESTIONS TO CONSIDER

- Are you ready to take the first steps toward leader-leader?
- Are you ready to take the first steps toward an empowered and engaged workforce?
- Are you ready to embrace the changes that will unleash the intellectual and creative power of the people you work with?
- Do you have the stamina for long-term thinking?

A New Method of Resupplying

Do you want empowered employees but find that empowerment programs don't help? We learned that empowerment is not enough.

Summer 2001: The Strait of Hormuz

Santa Fe was on deployment again eighteen months after Dr. Covey's visit. We'd gone through all the same inspections and predeployment workups as in 1999 but without much of the drama. I had a new XO as Lieutenant Commander Mike Bernacchi relieved Lieutenant Commander Tom Stanley and a new navigator as Lieutenant Caleb Kerr relieved Lieutenant Commander Bill Greene. Lieutenant Dave Adams, Lieutenant Commander Rick Panlilio, Senior Chief Andy Worshek, and Chief David Steele were still on board. During our training period, the new officers, Bernacchi and Kerr, quickly adopted the *Santa Fe* way of doing business.

Once again we were operating in the Strait of Hormuz at periscope depth, and we had a problem.

We had just completed an operation and were anticipating a replenishment port call. It didn't look like it was going to happen. Normally this would simply be a minor inconvenience because the submarine was loaded out for ninety days of operations at a time and we were not close to that limit.

Unfortunately, we had developed a small oil leak on a hydraulic ram that we couldn't fix at sea. Slowly but steadily we were using up our supply of oil and were at risk of having to terminate our operation early. Up to this point, we'd had a 100 percent accomplishment record in terms of making our underway days and assigned missions, and I wasn't interested in losing that record now.

The Strait of Hormuz is a busy place, and a submarine operating at periscope depth and slow speed has to constantly be on the lookout for traffic in each direction. As in the Strait of Malacca, supertankers are traveling in both directions; additionally, smugglers are running from Iran across to the United Arab Emirates, and of course, fishing dhows are omnipresent. By this point in the deployment, our section tracking team had been operating smoothly, and I was not overly concerned about keeping the ship safe. I periodically looked at the displays to assure myself that we were staying clear of all traffic, but I was not paying much attention to the specific ships we were avoiding.

We had an ensign on the periscope, Armando Aviles. Armando had graduated from the Naval Academy in 1999 and had reported to *Santa Fe* in February. He was brand-new. He was enthusiastic and unconstrained by knowing how the "real Navy" works. This worked to our advantage.

After listening to a discussion about our need for more oil, Ensign Aviles chimed in. "Hey, that's the AOE [a Navy fast-resupply ship]. Why don't we just ask them for some oil?" I looked at the periscope display and, sure enough, the fast combat support ship USS *Rainier* was transiting through the Strait of Hormuz several miles away.

The *Rainier* was a supply ship specifically designed with the speed to stay with the carrier battle group. It had deployed out of San Diego with the USS *Constellation* Battle Group when we departed Pearl Harbor. *Rainier* carried 2 million gallons of diesel fuel, 2 million gallons of jet fuel, and tons of ammunition and supplies. All we needed was a few cans of oil. Surely *Rainier* would have that.

There was a problem. All ship movements in the carrier battle group were directed by a series of messages. One message was the daily intentions message (DIM). If you wanted to resupply from *Rainier* you would request that it be added to the DIM. This needed to happen at least thirty-six hours before the planned event. One just didn't "call up" and get supplied.

Except in this case, we did.

Rainier didn't know we were there, of course, because we were remaining undetected. Even though we were in an identity condition that allowed us to be surfaced, we always practiced remaining undetected as much as possible.

My thoughts were, "It's a long shot, but why not? What do we have to lose?" I waved the flashlight around. "Go ahead, guys, see if you can set it up."

"I intend to break radio silence to coordinate a resupply from *Rainier*," said the OOD.

"Very well."

Nav called *Rainier* on the radio, identified who we were, and passed the Navy stock number for external hydraulic oil. Sure enough, they would supply us! Fortunately, Captain Kendall Card, a personal acquaintance of mine, had reinforced with his crew that they were there to support the ships of the U.S. Navy, and that trumped bureaucracy. I'd never heard of such a thing. Not only that, but the CO invited us to send over any crew members who needed medical or dental checkups beyond what *Santa Fe*'s Doc Hill could provide.

Rainier had a schedule to maintain; we couldn't delay long. If we didn't get surfaced in a few minutes, it wouldn't be able to stay around to help us.

The crew sprang into action, to which I gave my immediate assent.

From the sonar supervisor: "OOD, I intend to retrieve the towed array in preparation for surfacing. The sonar supervisor is the Chief in Charge."

Very well.

From the OOD: "Captain, I intend to prepare to surface."

Very well.

From the COB: "I intend to muster the small boat handling party in the crew's mess. I intend to break rig for dive, drain, and open the forward escape trunk lower hatch. COB is Chief in Charge."

Very well.

From our corpsman, Doc Hill: "I intend to muster selected personnel for dental checkups in the crew's mess, conducting watch reliefs as necessary."

Very well.

From YN1 Scott Dillon: "Captain, I intend to canvass the crew for outgoing mail and transfer it to *Rainier*."

Very well.

From the supply officer: "Captain, I intend to transfer the hydraulic oil from *Rainier*."

Very well.

We surfaced for a brief stop for personnel (BSP). Meantime, *Rainier* lowered a small boat, loaded it, and sent it our way. The small boat they used was called a rigid hull inflatable boat (RHIB).

We needed men topside and to open the main deck hatch to bring the supplies on board. Myriad various activities needed to happen quickly and in a synchronized manner. Here's where the training paid off—where everything we'd done paid off. There's no way I would have been able to pull off a plan for conducting this kind of operation and direct it piece by piece. You could call it speed of response, or reducing the sense-act delay inherent in organizations, or adaptability to change. Whatever you call it, the crew's performance allowed us to continue being a submarine in defense of the country rather than limping into port for a fill-up.

Not only did *Rainier* send the oil we needed; they sent newspapers and fresh fruits and vegetables (FFV) as well.

We brought the RHIB alongside. We loaded the oil, newspapers, and FFV and sent half a dozen crew members over for their checkups. I was a bit concerned about our vulnerability because we were on the surface in a highly trafficked area. Consequently, we shut the hatch and prepared *Santa Fe* to submerge on short notice. If we had had to submerge, the group on *Rainier* would have been there for a couple days.

Fortunately, that wasn't necessary, and shortly thereafter the RHIB returned with our crew members. We brought them aboard and submerged, ready to operate for as long as needed now.

Mechanism: Don't Empower, Emancipate

Empowerment is a necessary step because we've been accustomed to disempowerment. Empowerment is needed to undo all those top-down, do-what-you're-told, be-a-team-player messages that result from our leader-follower model. But empowerment isn't enough in a couple of ways.

First, empowerment by itself is not a complete leadership structure. Empowerment does not work without the attributes of competence and clarity.

Second, empowerment still results from and is a manifestation of a top-down structure. At its core is the belief that the leader "empowers" the followers, that the leader has the power and ability to empower the followers.

We need more than that because empowerment within a leader-follower structure is a modest compensation and a voice lost compared with the overwhelming signal that "you are a follower." It is a confusing signal.

What we need is release, or emancipation. Emancipation is

fundamentally different from empowerment. With emancipation we are recognizing the inherent genius, energy, and creativity in all people, and allowing those talents to emerge. We realize that we don't have the power to give these talents to others, or "empower" them to use them, only the power to prevent them from coming out. Emancipation results when teams have been given decision-making control and have the additional character-istics of competence and clarity. You know you have an emanci-pated team when you no longer need to empower them. Indeed, you no longer have the ability to empower them because they are not relying on you as their source of power.

QUESTIONS TO CONSIDER

- Are you limiting your leadership to empowerment?
- What programs have you instituted to supplement con-trol with competence and clarity?
- Have you divested yourself of the attitude that you, as a corporate leader, will empower your staff?

Ripples

January 15, 2011: Submarine Base, Pearl Harbor

I am sitting on the pier in Hawaii, January 15, 2011, twelve years after I took command of the USS *Santa Fe*. This time another officer is taking command and it's Commander Dave Adams. He was coincidentally assigned to command *Santa Fe* after serving an XO tour on the USS *Honolulu* and commanding a Provincial Reconstruction Team (PRT) in Afghanistan for a year. He wasn't the only *Santa Fe* officer to do that. Lieutenant Commander Caleb Kerr also commanded a PRT after his tour as navigator on *Santa Fe*. These officers are handpicked by the chief of naval operations. I don't think it was a coincidence that of the hundreds of candidates, three Navy PRT commanders came from one ship— *Santa Fe*.

Now, years later, I can see that implementing leader-leader on *Santa Fe* achieved two additional accomplishments that weren't immediately knowable. First, the ship continued to do well long after my departure. Since we embedded the goodness of how we did business in the practices and people, that goodness persisted beyond my tenure. The ship won the award for the best chiefs' quarters for seven years in a row and won the Battle "E" award for the most combat-effective submarine in the squadron three additional times in the subsequent decade. This compares with zero during the previous decade.

The other accomplishment is that we developed additional leaders in numbers widely disproportionate to the statistical probabilities. Both of the executive officers were selected to command their own submarines and were subsequently selected for major command. Both were promoted to commander and later to the rank of captain. The three eligible department heads were selected for executive officers and again to command their own submarines. They are in command now. All three were promoted to the rank of lieutenant commander, then commander, and two have already been selected for the rank of captain. The fourth department head was selected for the Navy's Engineering Duty Officer community and was also promoted to captain. Many of the enlisted men have gone on to positions such as chief of the boat or have attained advanced degrees and run businesses.

This is the power of the leader-leader structure. Only with this model can you achieve top performance *and* enduring excellence *and* development of additional leaders.

If the leader-leader model can work on board a nuclear submarine, it can work for you.

I worry that some readers will think of the list of mechanisms as prescriptions that, if followed, will result in the same long-term systemic improvements we saw on *Santa Fe*. I don't think so. In my work as a consultant after leaving the U.S. Navy, I have discovered that each organization is different and unique. The people making up the organization have different backgrounds and a different level of tolerance for empowerment and a different sense of comfort in emancipation.

Your mechanisms will be structurally similar, but the specifics will be different. For example, we found that one of the most important mechanisms for control was to change the level in the organization where an individual's vacation was approved. In your organization, it may not be the vacation policy. It may be the level at which discounts are approved for the customer. It may be the dollar amount an employee can obligate without higher authority. If you ask your people what authorities they would like in order to make their jobs easier, you'll definitely get some ideas.

Deliberate action is being adopted across the submarine force. It's known to the nukes as "point and shoot" and taught in the nuclear power training pipeline. Many commands enforce it and take it to heart.

"I intend to . . ." has also been spreading. I visited the USS *New Mexico*, a ship commissioned in 2010. While I was talking to the captain, the duty officer walked up to him and said, "Captain, I intend to . . ." That ship was running well.

As for "Don't brief, certify!" the language of "certification" as opposed to briefing has caught on within the submarine force, but for many it's just a different word for briefing.

For more information on how your organization can benefit from the leader-leader structure, I encourage you to visit my Web site (www.leader-leader.com) or contact me directly at david@turn-theshiparound.com. On the Web site, I offer several tools for building a leader-leader structure, including the seven-step process for effective self-assessment that we developed on board *Santa Fe*.

Ultimately, the most important person to have control over is yourself—for it is that self-control that will allow you to "give control, create leaders." I believe that rejecting the impulse to take control and attract followers will be your greatest challenge and, in time, your most powerful and enduring success.

AFTERWORD

Where Are They Now?

LIEUTENANT COMMANDER TOM STANLEY, XO on *Santa Fe* 1999–2000, went on to command the USS *Los Angeles* and was selected for major command. He commanded the submarine tender USS *Frank Cable* from 2009 to 2011. He is a captain in the Navy.

LIEUTENANT COMMANDER MIKE BERNACCHI, XO on *Santa Fe* 2000–2, went on to command the USS *Alexandria* and was selected for major command. He is in command of Submarine Squadron Four in New London, Connecticut.

LIEUTENANT DAVE ADAMS, weapons officer on *Santa Fe* 1998–2001, commanded the Khost Province PRT and went on to command the USS *Santa Fe* in 2010. He is selected for captain.

LIEUTENANT COMMANDER RICK PANLILIO, engineer on *Santa Fe* 1998–2001, went on to command the USS *Springfield* 2009–12. He is selected for captain.

LIEUTENANT COMMANDER BILL GREENE, navigator/operations officer (Nav/ops) on *Santa Fe* 1997–99, entered the Engineering Duty Officer program and is the commander of the Portsmouth Naval Shipyard.

LIEUTENANT CALEB KERR, Nav/ops on *Santa Fe* 2000–4, commanded the Nuristan Province PRT and went on to command the USS *Bremerton* in 2010. He is currently a commander.

SENIOR CHIEF ANDY WORSHEK, chief sonarman on *Santa Fe*, served as chief of the boat on the USS *Cheyenne*, was selected for master chief, and served as the command master chief of Submarine Base Yokosuka (Japan).

CHIEF DAVID STEELE, chief fire controlman on *Santa Fe* 1996–2000, earned his bachelor's degree, served as chief of the boat on the USS *Bremerton*, and served as command master chief for the Naval Submarine Support Command, Pearl Harbor, Hawaii. He is a master chief petty officer.

YN2 SCOTT DILLON, yeoman division leader on *Santa Fe*, was promoted to first class petty officer and chief while on *Santa Fe*. He is serving on the staff of the Commander, Submarine Forces. He is a senior chief petty officer.

SLED DOG, quartermaster on *Santa Fe*, successfully completed his tour in the Navy and has been honorably discharged.

GLOSSARY

Technical Terms, Slang, and Military Jargon

1MC Loudspeaker system allowing announcements throughout the ship.

ADCAP "Advanced Capability"—Mk 48 ADCAP torpedo. The main heavyweight armament of American submarines. Highly effective weapon against both submarines and surface ships. *Santa Fe* could carry more than twenty in its torpedo room.

ANAV Assistant Navigator. A senior enlisted man in the navigation department responsible for the preparation of charts and the safe navigation of the ship.

AWOL Absent without leave. Also known as UA, unauthorized absence. Departing your place of work without authorization.

BSP Brief stop for personnel. A quick entry into port during which the ship typically does not moor but meets a boat in the harbor to transfer personnel, mail, and, if fortunate, fresh fruits and vegetables.

BULL NUKE Senior nuclear-trained chief. Initially Chief Brad Jensen, who transferred without a successor. *Santa Fe* benefited greatly when Chief Mike Ciko came to be the bull nuke after the billet had been gapped for several months.

CAPTAIN By rank, an O6. The rank above commander and below rear admiral. By position, the commanding officer of a ship or submarine. What's potentially confusing is that the rank of submarine captain is commander but we call him "captain." Alternatively, the rank of a squadron commander, called a commodore by position, is a captain.

CO Commanding officer, "captain" of a nuclear-powered submarine. A commander by rank.

COB Chief of the boat. The senior enlisted man on the submarine. *Santa Fe* had a series of highly effective COBs: Mike Bruner, Robert Patton, and Jeff VanBlaracum.

CONN Raised area in the control room around the periscope station. Typically where the officer of the deck would stand watch.

CONTROL The control room. A room in the forward compartment, upper level, where the submarine is controlled, periscopes manned, and ship control functions executed.

COPY Radio download from the satellite. The download came unqueried at specific times, allowing the submarine to remain in radio silence. Also called "downloading" the broadcast.

CORPSMAN Medically trained petty officer or chief assigned to a submarine, called "Doc." Corpsman Don "Doc" Hill played a key role in keeping the crew healthy, which allowed *Santa Fe* to remain on station for extended periods of time.

COW Chief of the watch. The watch stander responsible for operating the forward mechanical systems such as masts and antennae, trim and drain and ventilation. Reports to the DOOW.

CSP COMSUBPAC. Commander, Submarine Forces, Pacific. The officer in charge of the Pacific submarine force from the international date line to the West Coast, a rear admiral. Responsible for preparing submarines to deploy. Also "SUBPAC" when referring to the staff as a whole, not just the admiral. Rear Admiral Al Konetzni was COMSUBPAC when I was assigned to *Santa Fe* and was highly supportive of our initiatives.

DEPLOYMENT Scheduled six-month tour away from home port. Submarines in the Pacific deployed to the western Pacific, Indian Ocean, and Arabian Gulf. *Santa Fe* conducted two deployments to the Arabian Gulf while I served as commander:

one in 1999 and one in 2001. During Operation Enduring Freedom some deployments were extended to more than nine months.

DIM Daily intentions message. A scripted message transmitted daily for the battle group directing all ship movements.

DOC See Corpsman.

DOOW Diving officer of the watch, also called "Dive," the watch stander, typically a chief, responsible for RAMOD—reaching and maintaining ordered depth.

DOWNLOAD See Copy.

EAB Emergency air breathing device. A mask, connected with an air hose to an air manifold, to be worn in the event that the atmosphere in the submarine became unbreatheable because of smoke or contaminants.

ENG OR CHENG Engineer or chief engineer. Responsible for the engineering department and the nuclear reactor. *Santa Fe* benefited from having Rick Panlilio as the engineer for my entire command tour.

EP Early promote. The highest fitness report evaluation. No more than 20 percent of the group evaluated can be ranked EP.

EPM Electric propulsion motor. A backup electric motor used when the steam-powered main engines are not available. The EPM drives the ship at slow speed.

ESL Equipment status log. A list of all equipment in a reduced or degraded status, needing repair, calibration, or maintenance. Typically runs into the thousands of items.

ET Electronics technician. An electronics technician was referred to as a "wire rate," meaning he primarily dealt with electronics and wires. Could specialize as radiomen, navigational quartermasters, or nuke ETs for the reactor plant.

FCS Fire control system. The computer system used to program and control the weapons (missiles and torpedoes) the submarine shoots.

FFV Fresh fruits and vegetables, when resupplied.

FITREP Fitness Report. Annual evaluation report.

FT Fire control technician. Fire control refers to control of "fires" in the sense of outgoing weapons.

INSURV A material inspection by a group of officers from the Board of Inspection and Survey. Their reports carry significant weight and expose the submarine force to "big Navy" observers.

KHAKIS The officers and chiefs taken together as a group. So named because they wear the same khaki uniform.

MANEUVERING A control room within the engine room where the reactor and propulsion plants are controlled. At sea, four watch standers stand watch in maneuvering: an officer and three nukes.

MESSAGE BOARDS Clipboard on which radio messages were routed; now done electronically via e-mail.

NAV OR NAV/OPS Navigator or navigator/operations officer. One of the three nuclear-trained department heads aboard the submarine. The other two are the Weps and the Eng. *Santa Fe* had two highly effective navigators: Bill Greene for the 1999 deployment and Caleb Kerr for the 2001 deployment.

NAVSUPE Navigation supervisor. A senior enlisted or junior officer watch station supervising the quartermaster. Stationed when the navigation picture was sufficiently delicate to require additional supervision.

NJP Nonjudicial punishment. A form of military justice that allows the captain to invoke near-immediate punishment without a trial by court-martial. Also called "captain's mast."

NUKES Nuclear-trained enlisted men. Nukes operated the propulsion plant and comprised over one third of the crew.

OOD Officer of the deck. The watch officer responsible for directing the movement of the ship and control of the watch team. The captain's on-watch representative.

ORSE Operational Reactor Safeguards Examination. A crucible event in any submariner's life! A comprehensive underway evaluation that tests all aspects of the submarine's ability to operate and maintain the nuclear propulsion plant.

PACE   Program for Afloat College Education. A Navy program for taking college courses while deployed.

PCO   Prospective commanding officer. An officer in the training pipeline assigned to take command of a submarine.

PD   Periscope depth. A depth shallow enough for the periscope and other masts to reach above the surface but deep enough to keep the sail below the surface to prevent counter-detection.

PNA   "Passed, not advanced."

POD   Plan of the day. Daily schedule and administrative notices.

POMCERT   Certification for deployment. A key milestone to allow the submarine to depart home port for extended operations against potential adversaries. Being certified means that the submarine is ready in all respects—training, manning, equipment, and weapons—to go to war.

PORT/STARBOARD   Said of watch station if there are only two personnel standing it. This means that each watch stander is "six-on, six-off." They stand six hours of watch and have six hours "off." It's a prescription for sleep deprivation.

PRT   Provincial Reconstruction Team. Civilian-military team charged with coordinating economic development, tribal relations, and governance in a specific province of Afghanistan.

QMOW   Quartermaster of the watch. The watch stander responsible for maintaining the ship's position. Stands in the control room and qualified personally by the captain, a highly visible and stressful watch.

RHIB   Rigid hull inflatable boat. The type of small boat that the USS *Rainier* used to resupply *Santa Fe* in the Strait of Hormuz in 2001.

SCOPE   Periscope. *Santa Fe* had two periscopes: an "attack" scope, with a narrow cross section and no electronics, and a "type 18" scope, with a wider cross section and comprehensive electronics suite.

SCUTTLEBUTT   Rumor, gossip. The scuttlebutt is actually a water fountain, a place where sailors congregate and share stories.

SSBN Naval designation for a nuclear-powered ballistic missile submarine. The USS *Will Rogers* was SSBN-659.

SSM Ship System Manual. Book of procedures for how to run the forward part of the submarine.

SSN Naval designation for a nuclear-powered attack submarine. The USS *Santa Fe* was SSN-763.

SSORM Standard Submarine Organization and Regulations Manual. The manual specifying the organizational structure and major administrative procedures aboard the submarine.

STAND-DOWN A period of significantly reduced activity aboard the submarine. The in-port watches are reduced to a bare minimum, and training and maintenance are not scheduled. Most crew members need to report for work about every other day. It is desired to have a stand-down period just before and upon return from deployment.

STRAIT OF HORMUZ Strait between the Arabian Gulf and the Arabian Sea (Indian Ocean). Forty percent of the world's oil tankers pass through this strait. The strait runs between Iran on the north and Oman and the United Arab Emirates on the south.

STRAIT OF MALACCA The five-hundred-mile-long strait between the Indian Ocean and the South Pacific Ocean. Runs between Indonesia on the south and Malaysia and Singapore on the north. A submarine cannot operate submerged in the Strait of Malacca because it is too shallow. One quarter of the world's traded goods pass through this strait.

SUBPAC See COMSUBPAC, CSP.

SUPPO Supply officer. The only nonnuclear-trained officer aboard the submarine. Runs the supply department. *Santa Fe* had two supremely capable supply officers in John Buckley and Chuck Dunphy. Sometimes called "Chop" for "Pork Chop" because their lapel pins look like pork chops.

TLAM Tomahawk land-attack missile. The Tomahawk was the primary tactical weapon we had with which to attack land targets. *Santa Fe* carried twelve TLAMs in the vertical launch tubes in the bow and could dedicate space in the torpedo room for additional missiles to be launched from the four torpedo tubes. The Tomahawk missile is very accurate and can fly one thousand miles.

TRE Tactical Readiness Evaluation. A comprehensive underway inspection that tests the submarine's ability to execute its wartime missions. The TRE involves shooting exercise torpedoes at friendly ships and submarines playing adversary roles.

UA Unauthorized absence. Also known as AWOL.

VLS Vertical launch system. Twelve vertical launch missile tubes added to the bow of the submarine. This was one of the differences between the original 688-class submarine and the "improved," or 688i-class, submarines.

WARDROOM Dining room for the officers. It also serves as a training room, an operational planning room, a meeting room, and if necessary, as the surgical operating room as well.

WEPS Weapons officer. One of the three nuclear-trained department heads aboard the submarine. The other two are the Eng and Nav. *Santa Fe* benefited from having Dave Adams as the weapons officer for both the 1999 and the 2001 deployments. Dave took command of *Santa Fe* in 2011.

XO Executive officer, Exec, the second in command of a nuclear-powered submarine. Would replace the captain if he became incapacitated. A lieutenant commander by rank. Tom Stanley was the XO for the 1999 deployment, and Mike Bernacchi was the XO for the 2001 deployment.

NOTES

1.   John M. Gibbons, "I Can't Get No . . . Job Satisfaction, That Is" (2009 Job Satisfaction Survey), The Conference Board, January 2010, http://www .conference-board.org/ publications/publicationdetail.cfm? publicationid=1727 (accessed April 3, 2012).

2.   Mercer, "Inside Employees' Minds: Navigating the New Rules of Engagement," June 2011, http://inside-employees-mind.mercer.com/ referencecontent.htm?idContent=1419320 (accessed November 17, 2011).

3.   "Employee Engagement: A Leading Indicator of Financial Performance," http://www.gallup.com/consulting/52/Employee-Engagement.aspx (accessed July 12, 2010).

4.   Skip Weisman, "Why 44% of Today's Leaders Are Unhappy with Their Employees' Performance," October 31, 2011, http://www .managementexchange.com/story/why-44-today%E2%80%99s-leaders-are-unhappy-their-employees%E2%80%99-performance (accessed November 17, 2011). Reporting the results of a survey.

5.   Department of Leadership and Law, U.S. Naval Academy, Karel Montor and Major Anthony J. Ciotti, USMC, eds., *Fundamentals of Naval Leadership* (Annapolis, MD: Naval Institute Press, 1984), p. 1.

6.   United States Navy Regulations, with change 1, chapter 8 (Washington, DC: Department of the Navy, 1990), http://purl.access.gpo.gov/GPO/ LPS52787.

7.   Theodore Roscoe, *United States Submarine Operations in World War Two* (Annapolis, MD: Naval Institute Press, 1988), p. 273.

8.   U.S. Energy Information Administration, Independent Statistics & Analysis, "World Oil Transit Chokepoints," December 30, 2011, http:// www.eia.gov/emeu/cabs/World_ Oil_Transit_Chokepoints/Malacca .html (accessed February 11, 2011).

INDEX

ABOUT THE AUTHOR

A top graduate of the US Naval Academy, L. David Marquet commanded the nuclear-powered, fast-attack submarine USS *Santa Fe* from 1999 to 2001. *Santa Fe* earned numerous awards for being the most improved ship in the Pacific and the most combat-effective ship in the squadron. Since leaving the Navy he has worked with businesses nationwide as a leadership consultant. He is a life member of the Council on Foreign Relations, and he lives in Florida with his wife, Jane.

<u>Global Certified Implementation Partners</u>
Our global certified implementation partners can help you
implement an Intent-Based Leadership approach in your
organization through bespoke training, workshops, coaching,
expert support and advice designed specifically around your
needs and context.

<u>In the UK</u>
Re:markable
(+44) 131 625 0155
Bonnie.Clarke@thisisremarkable.com
https://www.thisisremarkable.com/

<u>In Scandinavia</u>
goAgile
POC: Ole Jepsen, CEO & Transformation Advisor, goAgile
(+45) 5052 6212
ole@goagile.dk
http://goagile.dk/

<u>US and rest of world</u>
Turn the Ship Around, LLC
POC: Chuck Dunphy, Chief Operating Officer
(001) 941 408 0311
chuck@turntheshiparound.com
http://www.davidmarquet.com/

PENGUIN PARTNERSHIPS

Penguin Partnerships is the Creative Sales and Promotions team at Penguin Random House. We have a long history of working with clients on a wide variety of briefs, specializing in brand promotions, bespoke publishing and retail exclusives, plus corporate, entertainment and media partnerships.

We can respond quickly to briefs and specialize in repurposing books and content for sales promotions, for use as incentives and retail exclusives as well as creating content for new books in collaboration with our partners as part of branded book relationships.

Equally if you'd simply like to buy a bulk quantity of one of our existing books at a special discount, we can help with that too. Our books can make excellent corporate or employee gifts.

Special editions, including personalized covers, excerpts of existing books or books with corporate logos can be created in large quantities for special needs.

We can work within your budget to deliver whatever you want, however you want it.

For more information, please contact
salesenquiries@penguinrandomhouse.co.uk